Palatine to American Patriot

PALATINE TO AMERICAN PATRIOT

The Life of Garet Fiscus
1725 - 1797

MARY E CRAMER

Copyright © 2024 Mary E. Cramer

All rights reserved.

ISBN: 9798302002761

DEDICATION

This book is dedicated to my children Jonathan, Thomas and Michelle and to my grandchildren Anna, Erin, Allison, Emily, Calvin, Audenzia, and God's special miracle, Leon.
I want them to know the amazing story of their American Patriot ancestors.
Garet Fiscus (1725 – 1797)
John Fiscus (1745 – 1810)
Charles Fiscus (1759 - 1804)
Abraham Fiscus (1760 – 1834)

I also dedicate this book to all ancestors who emigrated from their European homeland in the eighteenth century for a new life in the British American Colonies, and who subsequently supported American independence in the Revolutionary War. They became American Patriots, and their courage helped form the greatest nation on earth.

Table of Contents

Introduction 1
CHAPTER 1: Rhine-Palatinate Origins 5
CHAPTER 2: Ober Saulheim 15
CHAPTER 3: Emigration 25
CHAPTER 4: Rotterdam Seaport 31
CHAPTER 5: Atlantic Crossing 37
CHAPTER 6: Philadelphia 43
CHAPTER 7: Lancaster County 53
CHAPTER 8: Westmoreland County 65
CHAPTER 9: Post Revolution 83
CHAPTER 10: Legacy 92

Knowing your generational story firms the ground upon which you stand. It makes your life, your struggles, and triumphs, bigger than your lone existence. It connects you to a grand plotline."

— CICELY TYSON, "JUST AS I AM"

Introduction

In the spring of 1744, Garet Fiscus,[1] age nineteen, and his friend Mary Magdalena Mertens, age twelve, left *The Rhine-Palatinate* region of Germany to sail across the Atlantic ocean for Pennsylvania in the British American Colonies. Garet's parents and his uncle had traveled the previous year. They were escaping poverty, starvation, onerous taxation, and the ongoing religious wars that had decimated nearly one-third of the German population and left the people destitute. Garet and Mary Magdalena could not afford their passage, so they traveled as Redemptioners under a contract to serve as indentured servants once they arrived in Philadelphia. They would be bought by the Mayor of Philadelphia, Benjamin Shoemaker, and sold a year later to a wealthy German Pennsylvanian, Conrad Reif, as his servants for a period of four years in exchange for their passage.

Obtaining their dream came at a price.

Like thousands of other German immigrants before them, Garet and Mary Magdalena sought a new life. America offered hope. They were so incredibly young to travel alone. Yes, they knew the journey would be perilous. They had heard of the dangers from their neighbors and friends who had traveled before them. Still, they were prepared for the hard work and grit it would require starting a new life in the Colonies. They were not deterred. The risks were worth taking.

The decision to immigrate to the British American Colonies was not an impulsive one. Garet's father had considered leaving Germany

---

[1] His German name at birth was Gerhart but he changed it to Garet after immigrating probably to assimilate and have a more Americanized sounding name.

for many years…just waiting for the right time. He would have discussed his plans to do so with his son Garet. Thus, America would become young Garet's dream for the future as well. Father and son were encouraged to emigrate by the many advertisements from British and American land and shipping agents. These advertisements were relentless in urging Palatines to sail on their company's ships bound for the Colonies. The recruiters described America as an Eden that was rife with religious freedoms, a beautiful climate, spacious frontiers, and the chance to make a prosperous living. For most Palatines, the Province of Pennsylvania was the preferred destination because there was an offer of land.

And so father and son left Germany…Gerhardt, Sr. first..

Garet and Mary Magdalena sailed the following year to the Port of Philadelphia. They were part of a mass exodus of Germans—more than sixty five thousand—who emigrated from their homeland to Pennsylvania during the eighteenth century. Most of them could not speak English so they hoped to lay down roots in one of the many predominantly German communities in Pennsylvania for comfort and companionship with others who spoke their language and knew their customs. Collectively, these immigrant Germans would become known as the *Pennsylvania Dutch* (an Americanized term for Deutsch).

A majority of the Pennsylvania Dutch were from the Rhine-Palatinate, located in the southwestern part of Germany. They were mostly an impoverished and illiterate lot. To high-minded, English-speaking British Colonists these particular German immigrants from the Rhine-Palatinate were derogatorily referred to as the "Palatines." It was an ethnic slur that carried a well-known stigma.

Garet and Mary Magdalena were Palatines.

Garet's father had immigrated the year before. Gerhardt, Sr. died within days of arriving in Philadelphia in 1743. The following year Garet and Mary Magdalena emigrated, but they survived the trip. Indeed, they would prosper in Pennsylvania over the next sixty years of their lives. Pennsylvania is where they would both die in 1797.[2] Together they would raise seven children–three sons and four daughters. They would achieve their dreams in America. But they

---

[2] Gerhardt's brother Frederich Fiscus and his family survived and eventually moved to the Carolinas.

would also experience great loss. Their oldest daughter, Barbara, was murdered by Indians in 1774. Garet and Mary Magdalena took in Barbara's only remaining child, John McCollough, to raise. That young man would grow to become successful as a Captain in the military.

Garet became a major landowner in Pennsylvania just twenty years after he was freed as an indentured servant. He purchased land in Lancaster County and Westmoreland County. Before he died, the Fiscus property had totaled twelve hundred acres: three hundred acres each for himself and his sons John, Charles, and Abraham. Their properties were all contiguous to one another. Some referred to the land as the Fiscus 'plantation' because of its size.

In Pennsylvania, Garet freely exercised his religious freedom as a Protestant. His faith was important to him. He was elected trustee of the Dutch Reformed Church and helped found two new Reformed Churches—one in Maytown, Lancaster County and the other in Mount Pleasant Township, Westmoreland County. Garet was also a community leader, having been appointed to the *First Grand Inquest Westmoreland County Court*, which was the newly formed judicial system. Integrity was recognized as part of his character. But most importantly, Garet Fiscus and his sons were American Patriots.

Garet had left the Old World of Germany behind because of political oppression. Now that he was part of the New World in America, he and his sons began to experience a different type of tyranny---but this time it was from the British. Indeed, the heavy-handedness of British rule became very personal to Garet. In 1773, the British tried to seize part of his property. They used a favorite ploy: "ejectionment." Ejectionment was a fictitious legal case the British would use to reclaim frontier land back from the Colonists. But the British did not succeed in their ejectionment attempt. Garet kept his land.

That pre-revolutionary attempt at property seizure surely must have firmed Garet's resistance to the British. He had worked too hard for what he had achieved. Pennsylvania had become his home. America was now *his* country. So he and his three sons—John, Charles, and Abraham became rebels for America's freedom.

The Fiscus men served the cause of the Revolutionary War. They signed the *Oath of Allegiance* in support of the American Revolution—forswearing allegiance to King George III and England. It was a bold act of defiance. John Fiscus, Charles Fiscus, and Abraham Fiscus enlisted in the militia on behalf of the American Revolution. And for their courage and acts of bravery, Garet and his sons would forever be recognized as American Patriots of the Revolutionary War.

Garet Fiscus is my fifth great grandfather. His son, Charles Fiscus, is my fourth great grandfather. Genealogical research on Garet and his family yields numerous historical documents and dates that provide an outline of their lives. But dates and documents do not make for a complete story. Only when history is transposed with their life events can we better understand the momentous times they lived through, the courage they showed in participating in the Revolutionary War' and the dangers they faced in staking out a new life in the perilous western frontiers of Pennsylvania.

Now that is the real stuff of a life's story.

Garet Fiscus, once a poor Palatine immigrant became part of an even bigger story…the making of the United States of America.

His is a story worth telling, as best we can.

CHAPTER ONE

Rhine Palatinate 1356 - 1695

Fiscus

The name is from Latin and means the basket in which money or taxes were collected. It is a root word for fiscal. Fiscus is the Americanized version of the German name Fishkus.

Garet's father, Gerhardt Fiscus, Sr., was born in 1695. He was German. More specifically, he was a Palatine. His region of Germany was the Rhine-Palatinate, or *Rhenish Pfalz*. It was located in the southwestern part of Germany, and its regional boundaries were France to the south and the Rhine River on the east. The western and northern borders changed over time based on the political fortunes of the rulers.

The people who lived in the region were called "Palatines." The term derives from the Medieval Latin *palatinus*, "of the palace" from the Latin word for the Palatine Hill, where the Roman emperor lived. In ancient Rome, a Palatine was a powerful authority figure. Later in the seventeenth century, the term "Count Palatine" was used for European nobles who inherited land in Germany and ruled over it separately from the greater kingdom. Being a Count Palatine meant having enormous power over a specific territory.

The Rhine-Palatinate countryside is strikingly beautiful, but it has a tormented past. From the sixteenth to the eighteenth centuries, the Palatines had to cope with constant wars waged by religious and political factions that left the people in hunger, poverty, and famine. Their farms, vineyards, and villages had been left in ruins and the Palatine people were destitute. By 1709, more than thirteen thousand Palatines had emigrated from their homeland.

HISTORY OF THE RHINE-PALATINATE

During the Middle Ages, Germany was part of the Holy Roman Empire. The country was divided into a collection of provinces, or *palatinates,* which were ruled by territorial princes, or Count Palatines (Fig 1). They were appointed by the Holy Roman Emperor to act as judge and governor over their palatinates. They had extensive powers and functioned like secular princes on behalf of the Holy Roman Empire, acting as stewards of the land for the pope.

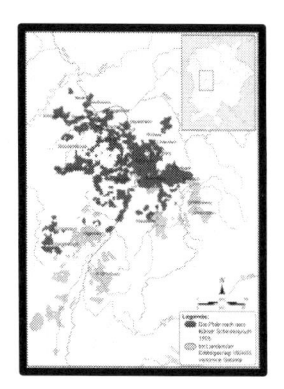

Figure 1

In 1356, the pope issued a *Golden Bull,* or papal decree, granting unique and powerful privileges to the Count Palatine of the Rhine-Palatinate. He was appointed to a prestigious seven-member electoral body that took part in the imperial elections of the Holy Roman Emperor. Thereafter, the Count Palatine became the most powerful figure in the region. To set him apart and recognize his special status, his title thereafter became *Elector Palatine*.

He was granted supreme powers to construct castles, issue coinage, and impose tolls. He could judge without appeal, and any conspiracy or rebellion against him was deemed high treason.

Heidelberg was the capital of the Rhine-Palatinate and where the Elector Palatine lived. Heidelberg home to the Holy Roman Empire's third oldest university, the University of Heidelberg established in 1386.

The Rhine-Palatinate was home to the Fiscus family.

BULWARK OF PROTESTANTISM

During the Middle Ages, the Rhine-Palatinate was Roman Catholic. And then came the Protestant Reformation in the sixteenth century. From then on it became the center of Protestantism in Europe. The Rhine-Palatinate drew Protestant believers from across Germany and Europe. It was a major gathering area for Lutheran and Reformed Church believers.

The Reformation began in 1517 with Martin Luther, who was a Roman Catholic monk and a professor of moral Catholic theology at the University of Wittenberg, Germany. Luther (Fig 2) was troubled by the Roman Catholic church's increasingly corrupt practice of Catholic clergy selling indulgences to absolve sin. The monies made from sales of indulgences were used by the pope to fill the church coffers and pay for the reconstruction of St. Peter's Basilica. The infamous slogan of indulgences sellers was: *"When in the coffer the coin rings, out of purgatory the soul springs."*[3] Salesman, like the infamous friar Johann Tetzel, would make parishioners "feel guilty if they did not seize the opportunity," reminding them of their parents and ancestors "clamoring for help" in purgatory and needing just one financial contribution to send them into paradise.[4]

Figure 2

---

[3] National Catholic Reporter. https://www.ncronline.org/news/guest-voices/peddling-purgatory-relief-johann-tetzel
[4] As cited in National Catholic Reporter taken from book *Martin Luther: Visionary Reformer* by Scott H. Hendrix.

Luther composed an essay of his concerns in which he detailed the Roman Catholic Church's abuse and corruption by clergy. He entitled his essay, *Disputation on the Power and Efficacy of Indulgences,* and nailed his essay on the door of the Castle Church in Wittenberg, Germany (Fig 3). In so doing, he was inviting interested scholars from other cities to participate in a debate on the topic. This was a privilege Luther held as a Doctor of Theology, and it was a common form of academic inquiry in the sixteenth century. Regarding indulgences, Luther wrote:

Figure 3

> *"There is no divine authority for preaching that the soul flies out of the purgatory immediately after the money clinks in the bottom of the chest. It is certainly possible that when the money clinks in the bottom of the chest avarice and greed increase; but when the church offers intercession, all depends in the will of God."*[5]

As to evidence for purgatory, Luther wrote:

> *"Of purgatory there is no mention in holy scripture; it is a lie of the devil, in order that the papists may have some market days and snares for catching money... We deny the existence of a purgatory and of a limbo..."*[6]

Luther concluded his essay with a question squarely directed at the pope.

> *"Why does not the pope, whose wealth today is greater than the wealth of the richest Crassus, build the basilica of*

---
[5] The Ninety-five Theses of Martin Luther, 1517.
http://reverendluther.org/pdfs/The_Ninety-Five_Theses.pdf
[6] Ibid.

St. Peter with his own money rather than with the money of poor believers?[7]

Luther's *95 Theses* were quickly distributed throughout Germany. The printing press had been recently developed so the Bible was now available to the laity. And it was printed in German--not Latin—so that believers now had direct access to Holy Scripture. They no longer needed to rely on the priest for the Biblical word. They could search the Bible themselves in considering the validity of Luther's arguments.

The most powerful argument of Luther's *95 Theses*, and the one that set the Reformation in motion, was Luther's assertion that God's grace was free. It should not be entangled with money or indulgences. Contrary to the Catholic Church's doctrine, Luther contended that Scripture alone was authoritative (*sola scriptura*) and that justification of the soul was by faith (*sola fide*), and not by works alone.

In 1521, the pope excommunicated Luther, but not before Luther had started a ground-swell movement that swept across Germany and the rest of Europe. Luther never intended to leave the Catholic Church, but the people had become spiritually awakened and enlightened by his teaching.

THE PROTESTANT UNION

Protestantism quickly spread in Germany and Europe. It had a significant role in accelerating the demise of the Medieval Feudal system in Europe wherein nobles and lords owned—by divine right—the majority of land granted through the Roman Catholic church. Protestantism challenged Feudalism by emphasizing the inherent value and dignity of each human being and his personal relationship with God—they did not need to approach God through the Catholic Church. Nor did the Church have the right to say only lords and nobles could own property. Protestantism empowered commoners and reduced the power of feudal lords, who had always

---

[77] Ibid.

turned to the Roman Catholic Church to maintain control over their serfs and grant them land. People had long been unhappy with the corrupt behaviors of the Catholic Church and now they were ready to see its authority challenged.

The Rhine-Palatinate became a major gathering location for those who had become Protestants. By 1530, the Rhine-Palatinate had officially adopted Lutheranism. In 1560, the jurisdiction of the Rhine-Palatinate passed to Elector Frederick III. He was a staunch Calvinist and thereafter the Rhine-Palatinate officially adopted the Reformed Church as its religion.

With so many Protestants in Germany, a formal military alliance, known as the Protestant Union (Fig 4) was formed in 1608 among the German Protestant states, including the Rhine-Palatinate, to protect against the powers of the Holy Roman Empire and defend for their rights. Frederick IV, Elector Palatine of the Rhine-Palatinate became its leader. The size of its membership of states made it a virtual bulwark of Protestantism. It was an important gathering area for many of the Reformation's leaders and followers, perhaps for reasons of mutual comfort and support.

Figure 4

Garet's father, Gerhardt Fiscus, Sr., was born in 1695 at the very epicenter of European Protestantism. The Fiscus family had been Protestants of the Reformed Church. It would remain the religion of Garet and his grandsons in America, as well.

SEVENTEENTH CENTURY WARS

In addition to religious struggles, there were on-going wars that left Palatines in famine and poverty. The *Thirty Years War* (1618 – 1648)[8] was started when the Roman Catholic Church and its armies sought to crush the religious freedom of the Protestant Union. An estimated four to eight million soldiers and civilians died from the effects of battle, famine, or disease. Parts of Germany reported

---
[8] Knittle, W.A. Early Eighteenth Century Palatine Immigration. Dorrance and Co., Philadelphia. 1937.

population declines of over fifty percent.[9] The Catholic Church armies pillaged and plundered. They consumed farmers' crops and wantonly destroyed individual property. Starvation and hunger became pervasive in the Rhine-Palatinate.

Then came the *War of the Grand Alliance* (1689 – 1697). The Catholic king, Louis XIV, claimed the largely Protestant Rhine-Palatinate as his own in order to expand his territory. His troops destroyed the countryside and sacked cities along the Rhine. In the end, the Rhine-Palatinate was badly battered but left outside French control due to an alliance led by England, the United Provinces of the Netherlands, and the Austrian Habsburgs.

From 1702 to 1713, the *War of the Spanish Succession* began when King Louis XIV again tried to extend his eastern border into the heart of the Rhine-Palatinate.[10] This war caused a great deal of instability. The people were burdened with heavy taxation as rulers demanded the Palatines pay for the expensive requisitions of the war.

By the start of the eighteenth century, the Palatines were in financial despair. They were desperately poor and on the brink of ruin. They had faced years of crop failures and decades of food shortages due to the effects of war. If matters weren't already dire, the winter of 1708 to 1709 was the harshest they had faced in over a century. It was so cold that the wine was reported to have frozen in its barrels.

MASS PALATINE MIGRATION

Queen Anne of England (1675 – 1714) (Fig 5) was Protestant. Her cousin, Charles III, the Elector of the Rhine-Palatinate was also Protestant. In the early eighteenth century, the Queen took great pity on the

Figure 5

---

[9] https://en.wikipedia.org/wiki/Thirty_Years%27_War#cite_note-FOOTNOTEParker1997189-29
[10] Palatine History. by Lorine McGinnis Schulze Olive Tree Genealogy http://olivetreegenealogy.com/ Copyright © 1996

plight of the "poor Palatines"[11] (who were mostly Protestant). She also wanted to help her cousin ease his people's suffering, so she decided to encourage Palatine emigration to England. To accomplish this, The Crown began advertising pamphlets and flyers distributed about the Rhine-Palatinate's villages and towns. The advertisements' intent was to lure Palatines to the British American Colonies by offering passage via the Rhine River to England, and presumably to travel on to the Colonies.

Thus, began the mass "Palatine Migration" from 1709 to 1711 (Fig 6). Garet's father, Gerhardt Fiscus, Sr., was only sixteen years old when the mass exodus began. He was at an impressionable age to witness the flood of thirteen thousand Palatines who left between 1709 to 1711, each carrying hopes for making it to the British American Colonies.

Though he was young, Gerhardt, Sr. surely would have been able to understand their desperation to leave. These were his neighbors and friends. He, too, must have yearned to emigrate and have the opportunity to own land and prosper in the Colonies. Afterall, owning land to a German was the mark of independence and success. The vestiges of feudalism still lingered in Germany. Nobles and the Catholic Church continued to hold the majority of land. The Rhine-Palatinate was largely an agrarian society, and for generations the people had labored in fields or vineyards owned by lords and nobles. The Palatine people were accustomed to demanding work, so the risks in leaving the Old World behind for a New World where there was land to own seemed very much worth taking.

Still, Gerhardt Fiscus, Sr. would wait another thirteen years before leaving the Rhine-Palatinate. He would be forty-eight years old when he finally left in 1743.

Figure 6

---

[11] Generally speaking the term "Palatine" referred to German-speaking people who migrated to America from the Electoral Palatinate in the 1700s. The term was used in a derogatory manner. (Otterness, P. Explorations in Early American Culture. https://journals.psu.edu › phj › article › download › 25606 › 25375

Palatine to American Patriot

Perhaps waiting to leave was better for Gerhardt Fiscus, Sr. As it turned out, The Crown's offer of emigration passage resulted in unanticipated and horrendous consequences for England. The sheer volume of thirteen thousand Palatine immigrants into England quickly produced overcrowding, depleted British resources, and led to domestic disturbances. The Palatines were forced to shelter in tents while they waited to learn their fate. And once again, they experienced hunger.

The Crown responded to the crisis, in part, by deporting back to Germany those Palatines who were Catholic. For the Protestant Palatines, thousands were sent on to Ireland to meet the British goal of repopulating Ireland with more Protestants. Only about three thousand Protestant Palatines ever made it to the British American Colonies—primarily to New York. The Crown's interest was to populate the Colonies with hardworking Protestant Palatines whom they judged to be less likely to rebel against British rule.[12]

Henceforth, The British Crown would have a very favorable attitude toward settling their North American Colonies with Palatines. In 1717, King George of England upped the ante for emigration by offering free land west of the Allegheny River. And so began a vigorous trade business in Germany. American colonial land agents, shipping owners, and The Crown[13] aggressively promoted emigration (Fig 7) using flyers, pamphlets, and newspaper advertisements that boasted of the rich bounty, spacious and available land, and beautiful climate in their Colonies. The Province of Pennsylvania was the most widely promoted as a favorable destination.[14] Emigration from the Rhine-Palatinate continued at a steady pace through the eighteenth century. Wrote one Palatine emigrant around 1720:

Figure 7

---

[12] Otterness. P. https://atlantic.fas.harvard.edu/Otterness%20-%20WP%2096026
[13] Knittle. W.A. Early eighteenth Century Palatine Emigration. Dorrance and Co. Philadelphia. 1937.
[14] Ibid.

> *"It was so great that, for a time, it appeared as if the entire Palatinate (the present Rheinland Pfalz or Rheinland Palatinate and part of Baden) might be depopulated ..."*[15]

To put in perspective the enormity of the Palatine Migration from 1709 to 1750, German immigrants accounted for one-third of the population in the American colonies, second only to the British.[16,17]

The Province of Pennsylvania was a major stopping point for Germans because there were already established and prosperous communities who were hospitable to their fellow German immigrants in terms of ethnic and religious tolerance. In fact, many of the German communities in Pennsylvania continued to speak in their native language. The new German arrivals to Pennsylvania would send a large flow of information back to their friends and family still in Germany to tell about their experiences and provide the names of essential contacts who could help them. Their information was considered reliable and it mostly corroborated what the recruiters from shipping companies had presented.[18,19]

Germany was the Old World. The British American Colonies were the New World.

And the future lay across the ocean.

---

[15] German Family Research Made Simple, Summit Publication, Monroe Falls, Ohio. https://homepages.rootsweb.com/~brobst/chronicles/chap2.htm#s6
[16] Library of Congress. Immigration and Relocation in US History. https://www.loc.gov/classroom-materials/immigration/german/building-a-new-nation/
[17] Marianne S. Wokeck, "The Flow and Composition of German Immigration to Philadelphia, 1727-1775," *Pennsylvania Magazine of History and Biography* 105 (1981), 260-61
[18] Diffenderffer, "German Immigration into Pennsylvania," 97-106
[19] Ibid

CHAPTER TWO

Ober Saulheim 1695 - 1742

Ober Saulheim in the Rhine-Palatinate, Germany was home to Garet's father, Gerhardt Fiscus, Sr. His village was nestled in a lush valley near the Rhine River, north of Heidelberg. The surrounding area was covered with dense forests and mountainous parts. There were acres of fields planted in wheat, rye, beets, and asparagus that surrounded the village. The economy of Ober Saulheim was largely agrarian. Farmers raised livestock, including cattle, sheep, and pigs. Ober Saulheim, like most small eighteenth century German villages, had a few craftsmen and artisans (e.g., tailor, blacksmith, and carpenter) who provided essential services to the community.

The region around Ober Saulheim was well-known for its vineyards (Fig 8). Since 1588, wines produced there have been considered among the best. The Riesling grape was first grown here. Still

Figure 8

today, the Rieslings from this region are among the very finest produced.[20]

There were numerous tiny villages that dotted the area around Ober Saulheim—Englsestadt, Wolfsheim, Alzey, Mainz. Many extended family members of Gerhardt, Sr. lived in these nearby villages based on the Protestant church records listing Fiscus names.[21]

GARET'S PARENTS

Gerhardt, Sr. (1695 - 1743)[22] was the father of Garet. He is the earliest Fiscus ancestor that can reliably be traced. He was born in Wolfsheim, Germany,[23] a small village in the Rhine-Palatinate. Gerhardt belonged to the Evangelische Kirche Engelstadt, Kr. Bingen (administrative district) (Fig 9). This was a Reformed Church that belonged to the Protestant church of Hesse and Nassau. It shared parish registers with churches in nearby Alzey, Wolfsheim, and Saulheim.[24]

Figure 9

Elisabetha Craemer was Garet's mother. She also was born in Wolfsheim, Germany; however, her family was Roman Catholic. She was baptized on September 6, 1699 in the Roemisch-Katholische Beulich, Rheinland, Prussia.[25] (Fig 10).

Figure 10

---

[20] Robb Report. https://robbreport.com › food-drink › wine › best-german-rieslings-to-buy-right-now-1235567822
[21] J. Kraft. The Fiscus Family.
[22] Some list him as Johann Gerhard
[23] http://files.usgwarchives.net/pa/1pa/ships/1743loyaljudith.txt
[24] Engelstadt Church Records via LDS microfilm (FHL INTL Film 1475629 Items 9-10 as recorded by Rodney Nelson Hoots and as cited by J. Kraft, Fiscus Family.
[25] Germany, Select Births and Baptisms, 1558-1898. FHL Film Number 585968. Ancestry.com

On the 30th of October 1724, Gerhardt, Sr. married Elisabetha Craemer.[26] He was twenty-nine and she was twenty-five. They wed in a Protestant church in Budenheim, Mainz-Bingen, Rhine-Palatinate, Germany (Fig 11).[27] Elisabetha may have converted to Protestantism before their marriage which took place in Gerhardt Sr.'s Reformed Church. One year after their marriage, Gerhardt, Sr. and Elisabetha moved to Ober Saulheim, about six miles away. It was here that their only son, Garet, was born.[28]

Figure 11

Gerhardt, Sr. is believed to have been a tailor.[29] The village tailor in Germany was considered among the "middle class." Most German tailors in the eighteenth century also had a small garden to help feed their families.[30] German tradesmen were limited in their mobility as explained below.

> *"If a town already had two tailors, and the town council felt that a third one was not needed, no other tailor would be permitted to become a citizen in that town. He may not even be allowed to just live there as a Hintersasse. Thus, many craftsmen either came back to their hometown to take over a relative's shop, or they married a daughter from a family in the same trade. Some married far away from home, perhaps in an area they had visited during their journeyman years."*[31]

---

[26] Sometimes lists her as Anna Elisabetha
[27] Joan Kraft. The Fiscus Family
[28] There may have been other children (i.e., Elizabeth (Schlosser married name) and Catherina (Kratz married name) but no other information is offered, nor are there records to confirm this information from family tree
[29] This supposition is based on the fact that his son Garet served as a tailor under indenture contract in America. Presumably Garet would have learned the trade of being a tailor from his father.
[30] https://www.familysearch.org/en/wiki/Understanding_Occupations_in_German_Research
[31] Ibid.

Little else is known about Gerhardt, Sr. or Elisabetha until they emigrated in 1743.[32] When they left Germany, Gerhardt, Sr. was forty-eight years old and Elisabetha was forty-four. They were headed to the Province of Pennsylvania in the British American Colonies, and they traveled with his younger brother Frederich Fiscus, aged thirty-six, and his family. They all sailed on the *Loyal Judith*.[33]

Gerhardt, Sr. and Elisabetha left their only son, Garet, behind in Germany.

GARET FISCUS AND MARY MAGDALENA MERTENS

Garet was born October 29, 1725, in Ober Saulheim. He was baptized in the Reformed faith of his father, based on those who have viewed German church records.[34] When Garet was still a child he would have begun his apprenticeship as a tailor and most likely with his father.

German apprenticeships for tailors and other trades often began as early as eight years old. (Fig 12) Young German boys who apprenticed as tailors were assigned to a master tradesman after confirmation around the age of twelve to sixteen years. Their apprenticeship lasted several years and at the end of training the boy was granted a *"Gesellenbrief"* or journeyman letter. Sometimes the journeyman would spend two to four years traveling from village to village working for various masters. Upon his return, he produced a "master piece," which was judged by all the master artisans of his trade in the area, after which he was then able to become a master tailor and eligible to join a guild. In many areas of Germany, especially

Figure 12

---

[32] J. Kraft. The Fiscus Family.
[33] See Ancestry.com Family Tree documentation for Mary Whittaker Family Tree.
[34] J. Kraft. The Fiscus Family.

larger towns, membership in a guild was required in order to practice a trade.[35]

When Garet emigrated in 1744 at nineteen years of age, he took with him Mary Magdalena Mertens. There are no drawings of what these two young people looked like, but Figure 13 depicts eighteenth century German peasants and their garb. This might resemble how Garet and Mary Magdalena were clothed in 1744 when they left for America.

Figure 13

Mary Magdalena was the daughter of Christiani Mertens (1712-1789) and Mariae Denn (1712 - ?). She was baptized on April 24, 1732, in Muffendorf, Rheinland in a Roman Catholic church with her parents as sponsors.[36] There is no birth record, but 1732 was probably also her birth year. In eighteenth century Germany, infant mortality rates ran exceedingly high. There was a sense of urgency to quickly baptize the baby within days or weeks of birth. And this would have been especially true for Catholic births because of their church doctrine of "limbo" for unbaptized children.

If 1732 was Mary Magdalena's birth year, then she was only twelve years old when she emigrated in 1744. Her parents did not travel with her, as there were no *Mertens* names on the passenger list for their ship, the *Phoenix*.

Why did her parents permit their daughter—a child—to travel alone with Garet Fiscus? Were Garet and Mary Magdalena like *Romeo and Juliet*, stealing away without their parents' knowledge? Or might Mary Magdalena's parents already have emigrated without her, just as Garet's parents had done with him? (Interestingly, there was a "C. Mertens" who traveled to America in 1742).

The fact remains.

Mary Magdalena was twelve and traveling by herself in the company of nineteen year old Garet. Obviously, they would have known one another before traveling together. Their families would

---

[35] https://www.cambridge.org/core/books/abs/apprenticeship-in-early-modern-europe/actors-and-practices-of-german-apprenticeship-fifteenthnineteenth-centuries/A8EB5454E454F1B8E95C028A407BE188

[36] Germany Births and Baptisms, 1558-1898. Record type Katholisch. Microfilm 176092

have been acquainted because they were both from the Rhine-Palatinate. German immigration in the eighteenth century was largely a group phenomenon wherein family members, friends, and neighbors from a village tended to travel together. Research shows this to be true.

> *"...eighty-five percent of emigrants traveled with family members, and ninety-six percent traveled with other persons from the same parish on the same ship."*[37]

There is a good chance that Mary Magdalena exaggerated her age to the ship's captain. She would have also claimed to be Garet's relative…a sister or even his wife. Garet and Mary Magdalena traveled as redemptioners, which was a system used primarily by families. Moreover, women and children on British ships had to be under the aegis of a male. Women were rarely listed on ship's passenger lists and such was the case with their ship, the PHOENIX. Mary Magdalena is not listed, so one cannot determine if she traveled as Mary Magdalena *Mertens* or *Fiscus*.

Garet Fiscus and Mary Magdalena did marry, but there is no documentation to reveal where or when. One year after arriving in Philadelphia, Mary Magdalena gave birth to their son John Fiscus. Did they marry before leaving Germany, after arriving in Philadelphia? That question is worth exploring.

GERMAN MARRIAGE LAWS

Legal age of marriage in Germany during the eighteenth century varied by state and religion, but overall the legal age was far lower in Germany than it was in colonial Pennsylvania. Prior to the Reformation, the legal age of marriage in Germany was strictly determined by the Catholic Canonical Law which allowed marriages

---

[37] Fogleman, *Hopeful Journeys,* location 1055.

for males at sixteen, females at fourteen, but legal guardians had to consent for juveniles.

After the Reformation, the German Protestant churches de-sacramentalized marriage and transferred legal jurisdiction to secular authority.[38] Each Palatine prince in Germany had the right to determine the religion of his own state, and the Elector Palatinate (where Garet and Mary Magdalena lived) had chosen Calvinism.[39] Thus, he had the authority to order local church consistories to decide all marital issues. Legislative power remained with the Protestant sovereign—usually the prince of the Protestant territory—but was exercised in accordance with the function of the prince as head of the regional Protestant Church and thus scripture-oriented.[40]

Moreover, the marriage customs in eighteenth century Germany involved proscribed and lengthy customs, referred to as *Proclamations* in regard to one's marriage intentions or engagements. Couples wanting to marry first recorded their intentions in separate books: civil and religious. They did so in the presence of their parents or guardians, several witnesses, and sometimes the local pastor. Then the upcoming marriage was "proclaimed" or announced publicly two or three times in each person's town of residence to allow for possible objections.[41]

Under certain circumstances if a couple needed an expedient wedding (i.e., pregnancy, already parents, emigration) one or more proclamations could be waived for a fee. This special permission was called a *Dispensation*.[42] Additional special permissions for dispensation were required for marrying someone of a different faith. This usually involved paying extra fees. If Mary Magdalena and Garet married in Germany before leaving, they would have paid the dispensation plus additional fees (i.e., one was Protestant and the other Catholic). Garet's parents had already emigrated by 1744, so the costs of

---

[38] WIKI TREE. https://www.genealoger.com/german/ger_marriage.htm
[39] JUDITH VON . T He History Of Marriage Law In Austria And Germany: From Sacrament To Civil Contract. Hitotsubashi Journal of Law and Politics 37 (2009), pp.41-47 ★
[40] Ibid.
[41] Baerbel K. Johnson AG® Research Consultant, FamilySearch. Marriage Laws and Customs in Germany
https://www.familysearch.org/en/wiki/img_auth.php/2/2e/German_marriage_handout_templated_jan_2017.pdf
[42] German Church Records. https://www.familysearch.org/en/wiki/Germany_Church_Records

dispensation would have fallen either to Garet, who most likely would not have had the money for that and travel, or it would have become the responsibility of Mary Magdalena's family.

PENNSYLVANIA MARRIAGE LAWS

The Province of Pennsylvania operated under British Civil Law until 1753. The minimum marriage age was twelve years for females and fourteen years for males under English Civil Law and by default, these provisions became the minimum marriage ages in colonial America.[43]

English Common Law applied in the Colonies until a state statute replaced or modified it. Under English Common Law the age of consent, as part of the law of rape, was ten or twelve years, and rape was defined as forceful sexual intercourse with a woman against her will. To convict a man of rape, both force and lack of consent had to be proven, except in the case of a girl who was under the age of consent. Since the age of consent applied in all circumstances, not just in physical assaults, the law also made it impossible for a girl under twelve years to consent to sexual activity. There was one exception: a man's acts with his wife (females over twelve years), to which rape law did not apply.[44]

Some historians maintain that colonial Pennsylvanians lived in an open society characterized by liberal, individualistic, and competitive values. It was no longer the old order, and there was an interest in populating the British American Colonies in a more expeditious and liberal fashion.

"The inhabitants acted to maximize self-interest in a market economy. The bond of lineage and European custom disintegrated in this unconfined country where the private ambitions and market-oriented desires of mobile, nuclear

---

[43] Dahl, Gordon B. (2010). "Early Teen Marriage and Future Poverty". Demography. **47** (3): 689–718. doi:10.1353/dem.0.0120. PMC 3000061. PMID 20879684.

[44] Lindenmuth, Janet. "The age of consent and rape reform in Delaware". *Widener Law Delaware Library*. Retrieved September 16, 2020

families took hold. Germantown inhabitants, for example, are depicted as "privatistic"—that is, having pragmatic, individualistic values rather than traditional patriarchal ways structure family behavior. Similar patterns evolved in Philadelphia and in the interior of Pennsylvania where settlers pursued "liberal," middle-class goals, emphasized individual freedom more than community concerns, and worked for their own material well-being. Contemporary observers overwhelmingly concluded that in eighteenth-century Pennsylvania most men and women married young. They ascribed the cause to the prosperous economy and the expansive freedom that residents enjoyed. To Benjamin Franklin, wedlock "is greater in proportion to the ease and convenience of supporting a family." More people joined in matrimony, "and earlier in life," where men obtained land to farm, learned useful crafts, or found employment as laborers. He conjectured that "our marriages are made, reckoning one with another, at twenty years of age . . . and . . . marrying early is encouraged from the prospect of good subsistence." Franklin's was not an isolated voice. Advantageous economic and social circumstances made it feasible for Pennsylvanians to wed early in life.[45]

Pennsylvania's commitment to religious liberty meant the Province avoided a rigid marriage code and instead allowed couples to marry according to the rituals of individual denominations. This resulted in more flexibility than the legislators probably intended, with some couples taking vows at home, others choosing not to marry formally, and, if a relationship failed, opting to self-divorce.[46]

There is no doubt that immigration influenced the marital patterns of Pennsylvania brides and grooms. Men and women joined in wedlock at younger ages during the early decades of settlement.

---

[45] Rodger C. Henderson. Demographic Patterns and Family Structure in Eighteenth-Century Lancaster County Pennsylvania. T H E PENNSYLVANIA MAGAZINE OF HISTORY & BIOGRAPHY Vol. CXIV, No. 3 (July 1990)

[46] Soderlund, J. Colonial Era Philadelphia. https://philadelphiaencyclopedia.org/time-periods/colonial-philadelphia/

Most men married for the first time between the ages of twenty and thirty-four. Women took husbands when they were fifteen to twenty-nine.

> *"Family norms structured marriage patterns not only in the Quaker community, but also among German Lutherans, Reformed Church members, Moravians, Mennonites, and Scotch-Irish Presbyterians. These groups regarded wedlock as a milestone in the transition from childhood and dependence to adulthood and autonomy. Legally and socially, sons reached maturity when they attained twenty-one years of age. Daughters became adults at eighteen or when they married, whichever came first had life expectancies of about thirty-five years."*[47]

In summary, the most likely answer as to when and where Garet and Mary Magdalena wed is Philadelphia and shortly after their arrival. The Province of Pennsylvania had more liberal English Civil laws and changed norms for marriage of immigrants. To gain passage on the ship, Mary Magdalena likely exaggerated her age to the ship's captain in order to travel under Garet's aegis—perhaps as his sister.

Either way, life in Ober Saulheim in the Rhine-Palatinate ended for Garet Fiscus and Mary Magdalena Mertens. They would never return again.

They sailed together to build a new life in the British American Colonies.

---

[47] Ibid

CHAPTER THREE

Emigration 1743 - 1744

Garet was only eighteen when his parents emigrated. He no doubt helped them with preparations for their journey. Travel advice would have come from their friends and neighbors who had made the journey and were now living in the Colonies. This first-hand information was viewed as independent and exceptionally reliable. Gerhardt, Sr. and Elisabetha might have even communicated with their German contacts in Pennsylvania to secure the indentured contracts needed to pay for their passage. The Palatines supported one another in this way.

Occupations and social standing in eighteenth century German society still had vestiges of the old feudal system. Ones' occupation defined his rights and obligations—people were born into a particular spot and expected to remain there. There was no upward social mobility. Gerhardt, Sr. had been a tailor, a member of the middle class, and like other craftsmen (i.e., weavers, tailors, shoemakers, bakers, carriage builders, and glass blowers) he probably owned a small shop in the village. Craftsmen owned a home and a small plot near the village for growing food for their family. So when Gerhardt, Sr. left Germany, his only child, Garet, would have been put in charge of his property and affairs. This might explain why Garet remained in the Rhine-Palatinate--to care for his father's property and business just in case Gerhardt, Sr. decided to return. Or perhaps Gerhardt, Sr. left ahead to pave the way for Garet's later arrival. The reason remains unknown.

When Garet emigrated the following year, he may have sold his father's property to pay for part of his own passage. (Gerhardt, Sr. had died in 1743). Or, Garet may have left his father's property in the care of another Fiscus relative in the area. Church records document many extended family Fiscus members living in the Engelstadt area.[48]

Either way, young Garet could not leave Germany without first dealing with the German law of manumission.

MANUMISSION[49]

The first step in emigrating from Germany was to obtain permission to leave the country. If aspiring emigrants had feudal obligations, then their permission would come from the local government. Most often, a simple fee of ten to fifteen pfennigs and a vote by the village leaders would secure a *"manumission permit."*

If the individual was subject to military subscription (draft) they would not be allowed to leave without paying a manumission fee to the government. This fee generally amounted to ten percent of the value of the emigrant's property.[50] That would have applied to Garet.

---

[48] Kraft, J. Fiscus Family. 2014.
[49] Aaron Spencer Fogleman, *Hopeful Journeys: German Immigration, Settlement, and Political Culture in Colonial America, 1717-1775*, Kindle edition (Philadelphia: University of Pennsylvania Press, 1996); locations 402-415.
[50] Werner Hacker indexed these records for many of the provinces of southern Germany.
Auswanderungen aus Baden und dem Breisgau (Emigration from Baden and the Breisgau), 1980 (FS Library 943.46 W29h)

EMIGRATION RECRUITMENT

There was a vigorous business in recruiting German immigrants to the British American Colonies during the eighteenth century. Colonial merchants and ship owners in England and the Colonies developed a profitable trade in transporting immigrants on their vessels. To load their ships with potential passengers, they would send agents to advertise with pamphlets and flyers distributed throughout the Rhine-Palatinate and elsewhere to convince them to travel on their company's ships.

The agents' advertisements (Fig 14) promised to pay for the costs (i.e., food, shelter, toll fees, and passports)[51] of the Rhine River boat trip that would carry them to the seaport of Rotterdam. In exchange, the recruited immigrants agreed to make their transatlantic voyage on the agents' company ships.[52] These agreements were not necessarily binding. Indeed, many emigrants broke their agreements after arriving in Rotterdam where they could perhaps negotiate with another shipping company for more favorable terms of agreement.

Figure 14

Since Gerhardt, Sr. and Garet both were headed to Pennsylvania, that means they were almost certainly recruited for emigration by one of the shipping companies licensed to serve the Port of Philadelphia. Recruiters for ships licensed at the Port of Philadelphia had a huge competitive edge with the Palatines. First, the Palatines overwhelmingly preferred the Province of Pennsylvania because of its established German communities. Secondly, licensed shippers to the Port of Philadelphia required no advance payments! That was something no other shipping company serving the other Colonies (i.e., Carolina, New York, Virginia) offered. To the impoverished Palatines, like Gerhardt, Sr. and Garet, this would have

---

[51] Sometime before 1739, the Dutch instituted a passport policy for German emigrants passing through Holland in response to complaints by local inhavitatns.t The passports had to be acquired by a "Subject of Credit and substance" who would guarantee the conduct, maintenance, and speedy transportation of the emigrants through Holland. Most shipping companies paid for this as part of their recruitment. Taken from Knittle, W.A., Early Eighteenth Century Palatine Emigration (Philadelphia, 1937), 47-65.
[52] Grubb, F. The Shipping of German Immigrants.

been a most enticing offer. However, there would ultimately be a price to pay for traveling without prepayment on these company ships headed to the Port of Philadelphia.

They would travel as Redemptioners.

RHINE RIVER TRIP

The typical itinerary for Palatine emigres was to leave via the Rhine River to the seaport of Rotterdam, Holland. The river trip was made on a boat (Fig 15) and always done in early spring so that the transatlantic voyage could be completed before winter. The Rhine River trip was long and costly. For those who could afford it, passage on the Rhine River boats cost anywhere from five to ten pounds sterling. In today's dollars, five pounds sterling is equal to $1,286.00. Children were half-price. Those who could not afford to pay for their river trip would negotiate with the recruiting agents who agreed to pay their costs in exchange for sailing on their vessels across the Atlantic.

Figure 15

The Rhine River trip typically lasted for several weeks, much of the time being spent in complying with the regulations of the various German principalities that existed along that great river valley through which they were obliged to pass.[53] There were at least twenty-six different stops along the way. At each stop the local authorities would exact another tax. The authorities of each municipality were in no hurry to have the boat leave. Indeed, they would delay the boat's leaving so that immigrants would have to disembark and use their own money to purchase food and drink and provisions in the city. It was not unusual for emigrants to have spent all their money by the time they finally reached Rotterdam.

The entire experience of the Rhine River boat passage was described by Gottlieb Mittelberger (1714-1758), an organ master and schoolmaster. He left Germany in May 1750 to make his way to

---

[53] https://homepages.rootsweb.com/~brobst/chronicles/chap2.htm

America. This was only six years after Gerhardt, Sr. and Garet made their trips to the Colonies. Therefore, Mittelberger's recollections would closely reflect what Gerhardt, Sr. and Garet would have experienced.

Mittelberger wrote in his diary about his entire ordeal in journeying to America. He did so to warn other German emigres of the extreme hardships in traveling to the Colonies. Below is his diary entry describing the Rhine River trip to the seaport of Rotterdam.[54,55]

"Under good river conditions, the trip down the Rhine from Worms to Rotterdam (approximately 350 miles) could have taken only four or five days of actual floating time. But there were many toll stations (associated with toll castles) along the way; maybe as many as thirty or so were active in the early 1700s. The toll castles belonged to territorial lords or to their authorized vassals. In addition to collecting tolls and searching the ships, the stops also delayed boats long enough to encourage (or coerce) passengers to spend money with the merchants of the castle. Consequently, toll station stops probably extended the river trip from Worms to Rotterdam from taking a few days to taking a few weeks, perhaps a month or so. The trip down the Rhine The toll castles belonged to territorial lords or to their authorized vassals. In addition to collecting tolls and searching the ships, the stops also delayed boats long enough to encourage (or coerce) passengers to spend money with the merchants of the castle. Consequently, toll station stops probably extended the river trip from Worms to Rotterdam from taking a few days to taking a few weeks, perhaps a month or so. The Rhine-boats that traveled from Germany to Holland had to pass by 36 custom-houses, at all of which the ships are examined, which is done when it suits the convenience of the custom-house officials. In the meantime

---

[54] Early Eighteenth Century Palatine Emigration. Walter Allen Knittle. Dorrance & Company, Philadelphia. 1937.
[55] http://www.danielhaston.com/roots/emigration/emigration.htm

> *the ships with the people are detained long, so that the passengers have to spend much money. The trip down the Rhine alone lasts therefore 4, 5 and even 6 weeks. At each of the customs houses*
>
> *Rhine River travelers who were emigrating were often presented with money and food by "pious countrymen along the way, many of whom regarded the pilgrims with envious eyes."[56]*

The arduous journey to the British American Colonies had only just begun. Emigres would have to steel themselves for what lay ahead. Crossing the ocean was "part two" of their journey, and also the most perilous.

---

[56] "Passage to America, 1750." EyeWitness to History, wwweyewitnessto history.com (2000). Published by Terman Society of Pennsylvania 1898 from Mittelberger, Gottlieb Journey to Pennsylvania in the Year 1750 and Return to Germany in the year 1754.

CHAPTER FOUR

Rotterdam Seaport 1743 - 1744

Once in Rotterdam, emigrants could embark on the ship whose company had paid for their Rhine River passage. Or they could negotiate with another shipping company for more favorable terms. When this happened the original recruiter would lose his money spent on delivering the emigrants.[57,25] It seems the business of recruiting passengers was a risky venture for a merchant shipping company.

The majority of the immigrants to the Colonies in the eighteenth century did not pay their way. Ordinary Europeans could not save enough in a lifetime to purchase their own passage across the Atlantic, much less that of paying for an entire family. The transatlantic passage fares from 1708 to 1756 were consistently

---

[57] Reber, P. B. eighteenth century immigrant ships - provisions, hardships, indentured servant process. 2019. http://researchingfoodhistory.blogspot.com/2019/10/eighteenth-century-immigrant-ships-provisions.html
[25] Gruber, Farley. The Shipping of German Immigrants.

between five and six pounds sterling per person.[58] This amounted to sixty-six day's wages for a skilled craftsman in 1744.[59] And that was for just one person. There was also the costs for wives and children. Thus, it is easy to see why more than fifty percent of immigrants came to the Colonies at the expense of others. This was made possible by alternative payment systems for impoverished immigrants. These alternative systems--*indenture servitude* and the *redemptioner system*—in their simplest forms allowed the impoverished emigrant and his family to sign a contract to work for a specified amount of time, usually four to seven years. In return, their owner would pay for their transatlantic passage.

The redemptioner system was particularly essential in settling Pennsylvania with the Germans. It has been estimated that two-thirds of the Germans who came to Pennsylvania came as indentured servants or redemptioners. Between one-half and two-thirds of all the white immigrants to the British American Colonies were indentured servants, redemptioners, or convicts.[60]

The indenture servitude and redemptioner systems essentially amounted to white slavery. There was already Black slavery in Pennsylvania—mostly Philadelphia—although it was not officially sanctioned by the Province of Pennsylvania. The presence of illicit Black slavery in Philadelphia existed because the seaport continued to be a stopping point for slave ships from the Caribbean, making ownership of Black slaves very accessible to Philadelphians. With the added presence of white indentured servants and redemptioners in colonial Philadelphia, a new hybrid labor system was developed in which the indentured white laborers, free wage laborers, and Black slaves all worked alongside each other.[61] The difference between them was that white indentured servants and redemptioners would eventually earn their freedom.

---

[58] Ibid. A notable exception was the ten-pounds sterling fare reported by Mittelberger during peace in 1750. However, Mittelberger's journal was an open attempt to discourage emigration and so may have been prone to exaggeration. See Grubb, "Morbidity and Mortality."

[59] National Archives Currency Converster. https://www.nationalarchives.gov.uk/currency-converter/#currency-result

[60] Ibid

[61] James Gigantino. Slavery and the Slave Trade. Encyclopedia of Greater Philadelphia. https://philadelphiaencyclopedia.org/essays/slavery-and-the-slave-trade/

INDENTURE SERVITUDE

Indentured servants typically signed their contracts (Fig 16) with American merchants or businessmen in Rotterdam and prior to embarking on the ship for Philadelphia. They may not have known the "purchaser" of their consignment or what the conditions for work might be once they arrived. The system was meant for individuals, so that a husband and wife and their children would each need to sign separate indenture contracts with individual businessmen. It was not unusual for children to be separated from their parents or even husbands from wives under this system.

The contract required the individual to work four to seven years in exchange for passage, room, board, lodging and freedom dues. Some Palatines traveled to America under this system; however, many more traveled as redemptioners because they came with families. Immigrants who had arrived via the indenture servant route were often likely to hide this fact from others once the contract was completed. Even though so many Colonists had traveled in this way, it was still not something one felt proud about as a Colonist.

The indenture servant contract was a standard printed form. It usually provided for the conditions of service and for the compensation to be awarded to the servant at the end of his term of service. The compensation varied. It could be land or money or other offerings.[62]

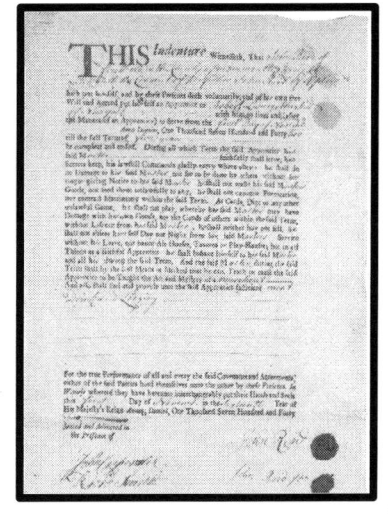

Figure 16

---

[62] Ibid.

REDEMPTIONER SYSTEM

In 1720, a new type of indentured servant appeared—the *redemptioner*. The redemptioner system was invented in the Rotterdam to Philadelphia shipping market and became universal among all shippers sailing that route. Hope & Co. were among the largest of the redemptioner merchants. They had a substantial business that specialized in recruiting German immigrants using the redemption system, more than any other Rotterdam merchant, likely because of their British and North American family connections. [63, 64]

The redemptioner system was primarily for families. Under this system, the husband had to be able to pay at least part of the family's passage across the ocean. The rest of the payment could be made in alternative ways after arrival. Redemptioners were allowed a period of time after arrival in Philadelphia to "dispose of their services to pay for the balance of their passage. If they could not do so, the ship captain could sell them as indentured servants to satisfy the remaining debt."[65]

Redemption was used extensively among German immigrants headed to Pennsylvania. It differed from indentured servitude in that it was a method used by families. This is as opposed to contracts for indentured servitude that usually applied just to individuals. The redemptioner system was a major recruiting tool for shippers licensed to serve the Port of Philadelphia. Other shippers serving the colonial markets of Georgia, the Carolinas, or Virginia preferred recruiting passengers who could pay for their own passage upfront or who had already signed indenture servitude contracts with land proprietors or businessmen in American before travel as a way to be assured their costs were covered.

Under the redemptioner system, an impoverished German emigrant could embark in Rotterdam as a redemptioner so long as he

---

[63] Keyser, R. American Legal History to 1860s. University of Wisconsin Press Books. Chapter 3. Indentured Servants. https://wisc.pb.unizin.org/ls261/chapter/b-indentured-servitude-in-the-colonies/

[64] Grubb, F. The Shipping of German Immigrants, p. 38.

[65] Keyser, R. American Legal History to 1860s. University of Wisconsin Press Books. Chapter 3. Indentured Servants. https://wisc.pb.unizin.org/ls261/chapter/b-indentured-servitude-in-the-colonies/

could pay part of his passage. Thereafter, he was under contract with the ship's captain or shipping company to find an alternative way to pay for the rest of his and his family's fare upon arrival. Most redemptioners brought individual property with them to sell once in Philadelphia and as a way to partially pay for their passage. However, if the redemptioner could not come up with the cash or complete the remaining debt after a certain period of time, he was sold by consignment to a local Philadelphia merchant who collected the amounts due from his sale. When that happened, the family usually wanted to hide that fact later in life.[66]

Several Philadelphia merchants made a very profitable business of buying and selling consignments. Consignments were essentially viewed as commodities. Indeed, the mayor of Philadelphia in 1743, Benjamin Shoemaker, ran one of the largest of these consignment businesses. It was he who purchased and sold the consignment for Garet and Mary Magdalena.[67]

BOARDING THE SHIP

Garet's parents (Gerhardt Sr. and Elisabetha) boarded their ship, *Loyal Judith*, in 1743. They were middle-aged at this point and may have saved enough money to pay for a part of their trip; however, the rest of their trip was paid for under an indenture servant contract with someone in Pennsylvania—with whom we do not know. Unfortunately, Gerhardt, Sr. died three days after his arrival in Philadelphia and there is no information about his cause of death. Nor is there information about what happened to Elisabetha, his widow. Elisabetha would still have been responsible to pay her own passage and Gerhardt Sr.'s as well. It was expected that a surviving family member settle the debt for a deceased relative if the death occurred more than half-way through the transatlantic trip. .

Garet and Mary Magdalena boarded their ship, the *Phoenix,* in 1744. They sailed as redemptioners, which means they sailed as a family…either as purported siblings or as husband and wife. They

---

[66] Ibid
[67] Grubb, F. Shipping German Immigrants. P. 44

did not have the financial resources to pay for their transatlantic passages so they used the redemption system hoping to pay for their passage upon arrival. Likely they took property with them, hoping to sell it in Philadelphia as many other redemptioners did. A portion of whatever money Garet and Mary Magdalena had with them upon departure from Ober Saulheim was likely spent on the Rhine River boat trip that took them to Rotterdam.

Their long, arduous transatlantic trip was about to begin. It was widely known to be the most dangerous part of immigrating to America.

CHAPTER FIVE

Atlantic Crossing 1743 - 1744

All sea-going passenger vessels in the eighteenth century that were bound for the British American Colonies were packed densely, *"like herrings so to say…One person receives a place of scarcely 2 feet width and 6 feet length in the bedstead."*[68] The average number of immigrants per ship in the German trade from 1727 to 1749 carried about one hundred eighty-five people.[69]

After boarding in Rotterdam, ships traveled through the Strait of Dover to Cowes, England on the Isle of Wight. British ships carrying immigrants were required to first pass a British custom house in Cowes before sailing westward. Here, the ship's captain would refresh the water and food supplies and make necessary repairs. Passengers had to present their passport documents again. The captain also was required to obtain permission from the British government to cross the ocean before leaving.

Another reason for stopping in Cowes was that The Crown required all passengers to sign documents ensuring loyalty to King George III and renouncing any connection to the pope. England did

---
[68] Ibid.
[69] Grubb, F. The Shipping of German Immigrants. P. 45.

not want to transport immigrants who might incite rebellion against them in their North American Colonies.[70]

LOYALTY TO THE CROWN

The British Crown considered the Palatines to be attractive recruits for their American Colonies. Their religious affiliation with Reformed and Lutheran faiths made it easy for them to sign the two requisite oaths of loyalty: the *Oath of Fidelity* and *Oath of Abjuration*. (Fig 17)

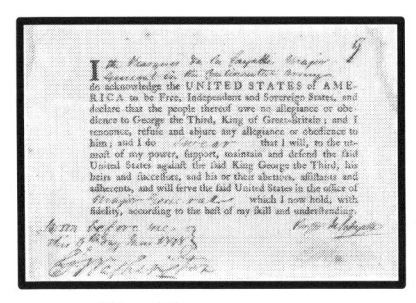

Figure 17

The Oath of Fidelity asked immigrants to disavow any ties to other monarchs and embrace the British King George. The text of the oath read:

"I A B do solemnly & sincerely promise & declare that I will be true & faithful to King George the Second and do solemnly sincerely and truly Profess Testifie & Declare that I do from my Heart abhor, detest & renounce as impious & heretical that wicked Doctrine & Position that Princes Excommunicated or deprived by the Pope or any Authority of the See of Rome may be deposed or murthered by their Subjects or any other whatsoever. And I do declare that no Forreign Prince Person Prelate State or Potentate hath or ought to have any Power Jurisdiction Superiority Preeminence or Authority Ecclesiastical or Spiritual within

---

[70]HistoryPin.https://www.historypin.org/en/explore/geo/37.77493,-122.419416,12/bounds/37.695104,-122.489626,37.85467,-122.349206/paging/1/pin/1191200

the Realm of Great Britain or the Dominions thereunto belonging."[71]

The Oath of Abjuration was anti-Catholic. It required the immigrant to abjure, or renounce, any previous connection to the pope. This Oath reveals the political and religious tensions that were prominent in England at the time. England's most powerful enemies were the Catholic nations of France and Spain. Relations with France were tense during this period. Moreover, settlers on the frontiers of England's North American colonies had accused the French Catholic missionaries of encouraging Indians to attack them. Increasingly Protestant England became intolerant of Catholicism in their North American colonies.[72] The text of Abjuration read:

"I A B do solemnly sincerely and truly acknowledge profess testify & declare that King George the Second is lawful & rightful King of the Realm of Great Britain & of all others his Dominions & Countries thereunto belonging, And I do solemnly & sincerely declare that I do believe the Person pretending to be Prince of Wales during the Life of the late King James, and since his Decease pretending to be & taking upon himself the Stile & Title of King of England by the Name of James the third, or of Scotland by the Name of James the Eighth or the Stile & Title of King of Great Britain hath not any Right or Title whatsoever to the Crown of the Realm of Great Britain, nor any other the Dominions thereunto belonging. And I do renounce & refuse any Allegiance or obedience to him & do solemnly promise that I will be true and faithful, & bear true allegiance to King George the Second & to him will be faithful against all traitorous Conspiracies & attempts whatsoever which shall be made against his Person

---

[71] Strassburger and Hinke, Pennsylvania German Pioneers: *A Publication of the Original Lists of Arrivals in the Port of Philadelphia from 1727-1808*, Norristown, PA German Society, 1934.
58 https://www.phmc.state.pa.us/portal/communities/documents/1681-1776/oaths-fidelity.html
72

Crown & Dignity & I will do my best Endeavours to disclose & make known to King George the Second & his Successors all Treasons and traitorous Conspiracies which I shall Know to be made against him or any of them. And I will be true & faithful to the Succession of the Crown against him the said James & all other Persons whatsoever as the same is & stands settled by An Act Entituled An Act declaring the Rights & Liberties of the Subject & settling the Succession of the Crown to the late Queen Anne & the Heirs of her Body being Protestants, and as the same by one other Act Entituled An Act for the further Limitation of the Crown & better securing the Rights & Liberties of the subject is & stands settled & entailed after the Decease of the said late Queen, & for Default of Issue of the said late Queen, to the late Princess Sophia Electoress & Dutchess Dowager of Hannover & the Heirs of her Body being Protestants; and all these things I do plainly & sincerely acknowledge promise & declare according to these express Words by me spoken & according to the plain & common Sense and understanding of the same Words, without any Equivocation mental Evasion or secret Reservation whatsoever. And I do make this Recognition Acknowledgement Renunciation & Promise heartily willingly & truly..[73]

CROSSING THE ATLANTIC

Sailing across the Atlantic in the eighteenth century was long and perilous. Space was tight, food and water were limited, and diseases like cholera and typhus were common. The journey took eight to twelve weeks. The diary recordings from Gottlieb

---

[73] Ibid.

Mittelberger on his voyage in 1750 describe the extreme dangers of the trip.[74:]

> "The third stage of the journey, or the ocean voyage proper, was marked by much suffering and hardship.
>
> During the voyage there is on board these ships terrible misery, stench, fume, horror, vomiting, many kinds of seasickness, fever, dysentery, headache, heat, constipation, boils scurvy, cancer, mouth rot, and the like, all of which come from old and sharply salted food and meat, also from very bad and foul water, so that many die miserable.
>
> Add to this want of provision, number, thirst, frost, heat, dampness, anxiety, want, afflictions, and lamentations, together with other trouble, as e.g., the lice abound so frightfully especially on sick people, that they can be scraped off the body. The misery reaches a climax when a gale rages for two or three nights and days, so that everyone believes that they will go to the bottom with all human beings on board. In such a visitation the people cry and pray most piteously. The passengers being packed densely, like herrings without proper food and water, were soon subject to all sorts of diseases, such as dysentery, scurvy, typhoid, and smallpox. Children were the first to be attacked and died in large numbers. There are deaths of thirty-two children on the ship.
>
> No one can have an idea of the sufferings which women in confinement have to bear with their innocent children on board these ships. Few of this class escape with their lives; many a mother is cast into the water with her child as soon as she is dead. One day, just as we have a heavy gale, a woman in our ship, who was to give birth and could not give birth under the circumstances, was pushed

---

[74] Passage to America, 1750. Accessed at www.eyewitnesstohistory.com (2000).

through a loophole in the ship and dropped into the sea, because she was far in the rear of the ship and could not be brought forward.

The terrors of disease, brought about to a considerable extent by poor food and lack of good drinking water, were much aggravated by frequent storms through which ships and passengers had to pass. The misery reaches the climax when a gale rages for two or three nights and days, so that everyone believes that the ship will go to the bottom with all human beings on board. In such a visitation the people cry and pray most piteously. When in such a gale the sea rages and surges, so that the waves rise often like mountains one above the other, and often tumble over the ship, so that one fears to go down with the ship; when the ship is constantly tossed from side to side by the storm and waves, so that no one can either walk, or sit, or lie, and the closely packed people in the berths are thereby tumbled over each other, both the sick and the well--it will be readily understood that many of these people, none of whom had been prepared for hardships, suffer so terribly from them that they do not survive."

Gerhardt, Sr. would survive the trip but die three days after arrival. Garet and Mary Magdalena survived their journey across the ocean.

CHAPTER SIX

Philadelphia 1744 - 1749

Surviving the transatlantic voyage was nothing short of amazin.g Captain Wilson of the *Phoenix* listed one hundred and ten male and fifty-five female passengers when he departed Rotterdam. The total number of passengers who landed was only one hundred and seven.[75] The rest either died or were left off at Province Isle to recover from illness. According to a publication by one family historian:

> *"Fiscus folk must have been a hardy lot. Ship captains were cruel and dishonest. Chest of required items were broken into and things stolen. One man wrote that he got on a ship at Rotterdam on 9-5-1747 and arrived in Philadelphia 4-5-1748. On arrival here most passengers*

---

[75] Notes of J.A. & Alma Fiscus Title: Typewritten family tree research notes, pp.21-54 of Fiscus Documents. Author: Jacob (Joseph) Aloysius Fiscus and his wife, Alma. Publication: Allison Park, PA, prior to 1972. Available through Mary Whittaker Family Tree on Ancestry.com

were owing money to the ship captain and someone here had to pay the bill." [76]

When ships first arrived at the Port of Philadelphia, doctors inspected the passengers to make sure they did not have any infectious diseases. Sick immigrants had to remain on ship a few days or go to a nearby hospital on Fisher Island[77] which was used as a quarantine station in the 1700s to isolate individuals who were ill, particularly during outbreaks of diseases like yellow fever. This practice was part of the Pennsylvania government's efforts to control the spread of contagious disease.[78]

The chaotic arrival scenario at the Port of Philadelphia in 1750 is described in graphic detail by Gottlieb Mittelberger.[79]:

"When the ship landed in Philadelphia, no one was permitted to leave except those who had paid for their passage. The others who could not pay had to remain on the ship till they were purchased by their purchasers. The sick always fare worst, for the healthy are naturally preferred and purchased first; and so the sick and wretched must remain on board in front of the city for two or three weeks, and frequently die. Only the sick who could pay their debt could leave the ship.

The sale of human beings in the market on board the ship is carried on thus: Every day Englishmen, Dutchmen, and High German people come from the city of Philadelphia and other places, in part from a great distance, say twenty, thirty or forty or sixty hours away and go on board the newly arrived ship that has brough and offers for sale passengers from Europe, and select among the healthy

---
[76] Ibid.
[77] http://zumbrun.net/genealogy/original-sources-the-passenger-list-and-ship-registry-for-the-ship-brothers/
[78] On the Other Side of Arrival. David Barnes. https://bldgblog.com/2009/10/on-the-other-side-of-arrival-an-interview-with-david-barnes/
[79] Passage to America, 1750. Accessed at www.eyewitnesstohistory.com (2000).

persons such as they deem suitable for their business, and bargain with them how long they will serve for. When they come to an agreement, it happens that adult persons bind themselves in writing to serve three, four, five or six years for the amount due by the according to their age and strength. But very young people, from two to fifteen years, must serve till they are twenty one.

Many parents must sell and trade away their children like so many head of cattle, for if their children take the debt upon themselves, the parents can leave the ship free and unrestrained; but as the parent often do not know where and to what people their children are going, it often happens that such parents and children after leaving the ship do not see each other again for may years, perhaps no more in all their lives. It often happens that whole families are separated by being sold to different purchasers especially when they have not paid any part of their passage money.

When a husband or wife dies at sea, when the ship has made more than half of her trip, the survivor must pay or serve not only for himself or herself, but also for the deceased. When both parents have died over halfway at sea, their children especially when they are young and have nothing to pawn or to pay, must stand for their own and their parents' passage, and serve till they are twenty-one.

When one has served his or her term, he or she is entitled to a new suit of clothes at parting, and if it has been so stipulated, a man get in addition a horse, a woman a cow."

PENNSYLVANIA LOYALTY LAW

Once the ship's captain had determined health status and how payment for each passenger were to be made, all males over the age of sixteen were required to walk in escort to the Philadelphia Courthouse (Fig 18) where they signed an Oath swearing allegiance to British rule in Philadelphia.

Beginning in 1729 the Province of Pennsylvania enacted this new law requiring an Oath of Fidelity and Abjuration. Philadelphia had received thousands of immigrants into their seaport, and the large influx of German speaking colonists alarmed the Pennsylvania government officials, most especially the mayor of Philadelphia. There was concern that the "large numbers of Strangers entering daily" could endanger Pennsylvania's "peace and security."[80] Certainly, the Province of Pennsylvania under British rule did not want rebellion or political disorder any more than did England. Thus, from 1729 until 1776, the Pennsylvania governor and the council required all foreign males aged sixteen and over to take their Oath of Allegiance to King George III and to renounce the pope immediately upon disembarking from their ships.[81]

Figure 18

GARET'S PARENTS ARRIVAL

On September 2, 1743, Gerhardt Fiscus, Sr. and his brother Frederich[82] walked from their ship the *Loyal Judith* to the Philadelphia

---

[80] https://www.phmc.state.pa.us/portal/communities/documents/1681-1776/oaths-fidelity.html
[81] Pennsylvania Historical Museum.
https://www.phmc.state.pa.us/portal/communities/documents/1681-1776/oaths-fidelity.html
[82] In 1747, Frederich Fiscus and his wife Elizabeth (Schwind) moved to Germantown, PA to a farm in Lancaster Couty and settled in Conestoga Township. Elizabeth died in 1750 and Frederich sold his farm and moved across the border into Frederick County, Maryland along the Susquehannah River and lived with his daughter and her husband Michael and Anna Hauser. In 1759 – 1762 Frederick and the Hausers sold their land and moved to North Carolina in what is now Forsyth County. Source: Owens County Cousins, Vol II, 1 September 1997. P 521.

Courthouse and signed another loyalty oath, which was similar in wording to the Oath they had signed in Cowles, England. This particular oath was required by Pennsylvania law to also ensure loyalty to England. Gerhardt, Sr. signed with his "mark" as recorded in the Captain's Log, List C found in Figure 19 (see the left column and about half-way down the page). It is not clear why Gerhardt, Sr. used a "mark" for his signature. Perhaps he was illiterate. Many Palatines were illiterate. Or maybe he was just too sick to sign. Indeed, Gerhardt Sr. *was* sick but not enough that he could not walk to the Courthouse through sheer force of will. Just three days later Gerhardt, Sr. died. It is probable that the rigors of transatlantic passage combined with the presence of rampant contagious diseases on the ships—typhus, yellow fever, dysentery—could have been the cause since he presumably departed Germany in reasonable health. Or, he might have had a health condition such as heart disease that worsened on the stressful transatlantic voyage, resulting in his death.

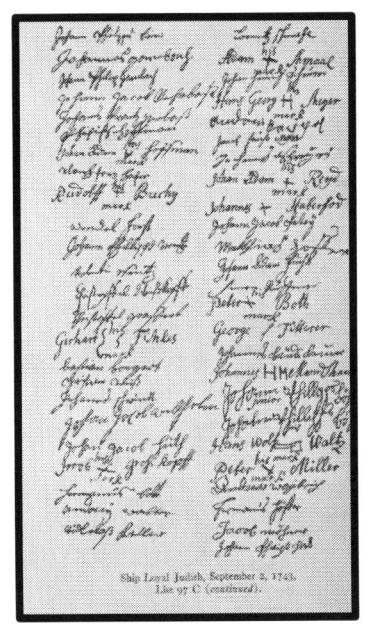

Figure 19

There is no documentation to be found about Elisabetha Fiscus and what happened to her after the death of Gerhardt, Sr. She would have certainly been required to fulfill her own indenture servitude contract as well as Gerhardt, Sr.'s, which was probably a period of four to six years. After that was completed, perhaps her brother-in-law, Frederich and his family cared for her in her later years.[83,84] Interestingly, there is no indication that she ever lived with Garet and Mary Magdalena, although this may have been the case despite lack of records.

---

[83] https://freepages.rootsweb.com/~cale2cales/genealogy/ship93.htm
[84] http://files.usgwarchives.net/pa/1pa/ships/1743loyaljudith.txt

GARET AND MARY MAGDALENA ARRIVAL

Garet and Mary Magdalena arrived at the Port of Philadelphia on their ship, the *Phoenix* on October 8, 1744. Garet made the same walk to the Courthouse that his father had done the year before. There he signed the Oath using his given German name "Gerhart." Figure 20 depicts his actual signature, found on the left column and about one-third of the way down. The original entry notes preceding his signature read:

"*The Foreigners whose names are underwritten, imported in the Phoenix, William Wilson, Capt, from Rotterdam, & last from Cowes, did this day take the foregoing Oaths to the Government.*"[85]

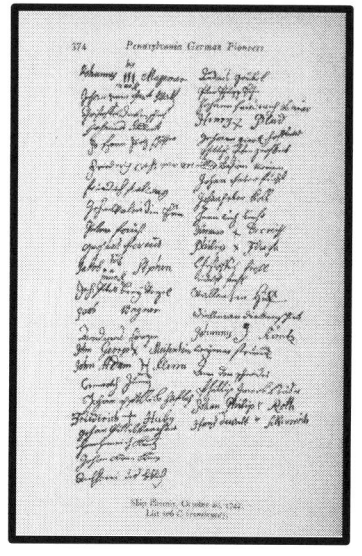

Figure 20

REDEMPTIONERS TO INDENTURED SERVANTS

Garet and Mary Magdalena were redemptioners…specifically *Palatine* redemptioners. The pejorative term "Palatine" was widely used by the British to describe those from the Rhine-Palatinate because they were mostly poor, illiterate, and non-English speaking. Garet and Mary Magdalena, not having funds to pay for the remainder of their passage, were purchased as "consignment property."

Consignments were essentially commodities that were bought by prominent businessmen and resold for a profit. The consignment for Garet and Mary Magdalena was purchased by Benjamin Shoemaker, Mayor of Philadelphia. Mr. Shoemaker had been born in

---

[85] Pennsylvania German Archives.
https://archive.org/details/pennsylvaniagerm03penn_2/page/355/mode/1up?q=fiscus&view=theater

Germantown, Pennsylvania but his father was from the Rhine-Palatinate. Mr. Shoemaker gave preference to buying Palatine consignments. The Mayor had made a profitable and well-known business of this, and it is believed most of the consignments he purchased were from his father's region of Germany out of partiality for those of his own background.

Garet and Mary Magdalena spent their first year in Philadelphia under the auspices of Mayor Shoemaker. They used their "grace period" to come up with funds for their debt—perhaps selling some property they brought or attempting to borrow money from friends or relatives in Pennsylvania, or perhaps even setting up shop as a tailor. It was also during that first year that Mary Magdalena gave birth at age thirteen. On October 29, 1745, their first child, Johann (John) Fiscus was born. John was baptized on November 3, 1745, in the German Reformed Church in Philadelphia.

Figure 21

Despite their efforts to pay off debt, Garet and Mary Magdalena were unsuccessful. On December 7, 1745, they were sold by Mayor Shoemaker to a wealthy businessman and landowner, Conrad Reif[86] (Fig 21). The indenture contract bought Garet's services as a tailor and Mary Magdalena as a domestic servant for a period of four years. In return, Conrad Reif agreed to pay Mayor Shoemaker twenty-one pounds for Garet and Mary Magdalena's costs of transatlantic passage.

Conrad Reif was an interesting fellow. He had immigrated to Philadelphia in 1730 - 1731[87] from the Rhine-Palatinate. He quickly became a prominent citizen of Philadelphia and a wealthy land holder in western Pennsylvania.[88] Mr. Reif was a "naturalized inhabitant of

---

[86] Pennsylvania Magazine of History and Biography, 1907, Vol. 31, No. 1.: 83-192
[87] U.S. and Canada, Passenger and Immigration Lists Index, 1500s-1900s. https://www.ancestry.com/search/collections/7486/records/3490259?tid=&pid=&queryid=32fcf7f a-b2ab-4d21-80f1-82fd7b01f98e&_phsrc=ZkF44&_phstart=successSource
[88] https://www.loc.gov › item › usrep001001a

the Province of Pennsylvania" and thereby had been granted the ability to "hold lands." [89,60] (Fig 22)

Mr. Reif purchased Garet's contract because they were both from the same region and because he needed a tailor. German immigrants largely supported one another in Pennsylvania, and those who could afford it would often purchase indenture contracts of immigrants from their own region of origin.

Figure 22

Conrad Reif was a man of stature in Philadelphia and had just been granted eighty acres in Lancaster County prior to indenturing Garet. Lancaster County is adjacent to Philadelphia so it is curious to think how Mr. Reif managed his property during this time in Philadelphia. Perhaps Garet helped him with that property. Fiscus family documents claim that Mr. Reif's home in Philadelphia was next to the home of Benjamin Franklin.[90] (Fig 23).

Figure 23

In many ways it was fortunate that Garet and Mary Magdalena lived in Philadelphia, first under Mayor Shoemaker and then serving a wealthy businessman, Conrad Reif. The benefits of living in relatively privileged homes and in Philadelphia—considered a culturally rich city—must have included the opportunity, even expectation, of learning English as well as getting accustomed to new colonial ways. It might have even allowed the chance to make influential friendships. Indeed, Fiscus family lore is that there was a marriage between a member of the Franklin family and the Fiscus family.[91]

---

[89] 1730 Naturalization Act. https://www.anamericanfamilyhistory.com/Bachtel Family/1730Naturalization.html
[90] The Fiscus Family. J. Kraft
[91] Ibid.

Palatine to American Patriot

When Garet arrived in America, he had already mastered his tailoring skills and apparently was good enough that a wealthy businessman would pay for his services. Tailoring was a valuable talent. In colonial America, men's clothing was quite ornate and detailed (Fig 24) so tailoring was a respected trade and in high demand. Tailors were the largest trade in terms of craftsmen in urban colonial America. Most colonists bought their clothes and few were so self-sufficient that they could weave the cloth, cut the pattern, carve the buttons, and hand sew the pieces together. Demand for clothing was so strong that cloth was America's largest import before the Revolution. Almost everybody in the eighteenth century—wealthy or poor--required a tailor.[92]

Figure 24

Mary Magdalena's servitude was for household help (Fig 25). Her young son, John, would have been present with her as she completed her daily work in Mr. Reif's household.

Figure 25

LIFE IN PHILADELPHIA 1744 - 1749

Philadelphia was known in colonial times as the "Athens of America" because of its rich cultural life and generally more lax moral codes (Fig 26). But like most American colonial cities, it was dirty. The streets were dirt and mud, strewn with garbage and animal litter. Still, Philadelphia was a bustling city because of its seaport, which mostly traded with West Indies ships. The seaport was also a busy point of arrival for thousands of German immigrants.

Figure 26

---

[92] Crews, E. Tailor Made for History:
https://research.colonialwilliamsburg.org/Foundation/journal/Autumn05/tailor.cfm

There was a certain "liberality of principles" and "freedom of expression" that prevailed in Philadelphia.[93] A variety of intellectual and educational institutions existed there. For example, the College of Philadelphia was established in 1755 and was the only nondenominational college of the colonial period (ultimately becoming the University of Pennsylvania). Arts and sciences flourished in Philadelphia, and it is said that the public buildings of Philadelphia were the "marvel of the colonies."[94] Newspapers and magazines abounded—most notably the *Philadelphia Gazette* owned by Benjamin Franklin. Philadelphia had the first hospital, first library, and first insurance company in America. Of course, the city's most famous resident was Benjamin Franklin who had arrived in Philadelphia in 1723.

Philadelphia was a cosmopolitan atmosphere that Garet and Mary Magdalena could never have imagined, having come from such rural, humble, and Old World roots as the Rhine-Palatinate. It must have felt invigorating and at the same time disorienting to them. But Garet was still longing to live out his dream. He yearned to own land.

That part of his dream would have to wait until they fulfilled their indenture servitude contract.

---

[93] https://www.phmc.state.pa.us/portal/communities/pa-history/1681-1776.html
[94] Ibid.

CHAPTER SEVEN

Lancaster County 1750 - 1768

Pennsylvania was officially established by William Penn, a newly converted aristocratic Quaker. He received the land grant for Pennsylvania in payment for a personal debt owed by the King to his father. The land he received was rich with natural resources including two river valleys, extensive forests, and a substantial portion of the Appalachian Mountains. Penn made several trips to Europe, especially Germany and the Rhine-Palatinate to recruit immigrants who could populate his new land. Many of those recruited were or became Quakers. Philadelphia quickly became a refuge for Quakers in the New World.

The government of Pennsylvania was based on Penn's Quaker beliefs. He allowed his colonists to govern themselves by establishing a Colony Council. Penn (and later his sons and grandsons who governed after him) established laws that provided for children's education. They banned slavery in the Province of Pennsylvania (although it still existed mostly in Philadelphia). Most notably, Penn's government created the means for indentured servants to become free men and citizens in the Province of Pennsylvania after completing their service term.

Penn's government style attracted many immigrants and very quickly, causing its growth to surpass the population of New York Colony. His Quaker pacifist style also facilitated several treaties with the local Native Americans, who mostly remained peaceful throughout the pre-Revolutionary years.[95]

GARET'S RELIGION

Religion was a large part of Garet's life. Like his father, he had belonged to the Evangelishe Kirche in Ober Saulheim—a Reformed Church. After he arrived in the Province of Pennsylvania, he would found and build two new Reformed Churches in the communities where he lived—Maytown, Lancaster County and in Mount Pleasant Township, Westmoreland County.

The Reformed Church of eighteenth century America adhered to the *Heidelberg Catechism*. The Catechism had been written in the sixteenth century at the request of Elector Frederick III, ruler of the most influential German province, the Rhine-Palatinate, from 1559 to 1576. Being a pious Christian prince, Frederick III commissioned a professor of theology at the Heidelberg University, and with the advice of the entire theological faculty, to prepare a Catechism for instructing the youth and for guiding pastors and teachers in the Reformed Church. It came to be known as *The Heidelberg Catechism* and was adopted by a Synod in Heidelberg and published in German with a preface by Frederick III, dated January 19, 1563.[96]

The Heidelberg Catechism is formatted into fifty-two sections, so that a section of the Catechism could be explained to the churches each Sunday of the year. It is presented in a question and answer

---

[95] https://www.reference.com/history-geography/daily-life-like-colonial-pennsylvania-cd0191b5fc99b141
[96] Westminster Theological Seminary. ttps://students.wts.edu/resources/creeds/heidelberg.html

format and referenced with Biblical verses. It's very first question was:

> 1. Q. *What is your only comfort in life and death?*
>
> A. *That I am not my own,[1] but belong with body and soul, both in life and in death,[2] to my faithful Saviour Jesus Christ.[3] He has fully paid for all my sins with His precious blood, and has set me free from all the power of the devil.[5] He also preserves me in such a way[6] that without the will of my heavenly Father not a hair can fall from my head;[7] indeed, all things must work together for my salvation.[8] Therefore, by His Holy Spirit He also assures me of eternal life[9] and makes me heartily willing and ready from now on to live for Him.[10]*
>
> [1] I Cor. 6:19, 20 [2] Rom. 14:7-9. [3] I Cor. 3:23; Tit. 2:14. [4] I Pet. 1:18, 19; I John 1:7; 2:2. [5] John 8:34-36; Heb. 2:14, 15; I John 3:8. [6] John 6:39, 40; 10:27-30; II Thess. 3:3; I Pet. 1:5. [7] Matt. 10:29-31; Luke 21:16-18. [8] Rom. 8:28. [9] Rom. 8:15, 16; II Cor. 1:21, 22; 5:5; Eph. 1:13, 14. [10] Rom. 8:14.

The Heidelberg Catechism was founded on important Protestant tenets: 1) the church belonged to the people and not to the pope, 2) people had direct access to God through scripture and prayer, and 3) a priest was not needed to approach God or grant forgiveness. *The Heidelberg Catechism* taught that salvation was from God's grace, and not only from our works.

It is clear that the Reformed Church was central to Garet's life and its tenets had formed his world view and how he would live his life in the Colonies.

LIFE IN LANCASTER COUNTY

It has been said the most important factors in understanding our Pennsylvania German colonist ancestors during the eighteenth century were: 1) their strong desire for owning land, and 2) being part of a cohesive community.[97] In his book, *Hopeful Journeys*, Aaron Fogelman says that German-speaking immigrants in the eighteenth century were "hypersensitive to political matters involving land."[98] They had survived in land-starved Germany by being united against the oppressive political powers of the Catholic Church and of overreaching rulers. In the American Colonies the German immigrants relied on their spirit of collective behavior to survive and support one another. Fogelman reasons that most Pennsylvania Germans had come as indentured servants or redemptioners to pay for their passage, and they had contracted with other Germans with whom they had a connection, such as family or people from their neighboring villages. Having this connection meant they wanted to stay in the good graces of the German Pennsylvania community and seldom reneged on their contracts. They needed cooperation to survive in the foreign land.[99]

Garet fulfilled his indenture contract in 1749 and immediately set out to purchase land. He, Mary Magdalena, and son John moved to Lancaster County, a rural area of Pennsylvania and not far from Philadelphia. The land in Lancaster County was mostly frontier. His first recorded location in Lancaster County was Manchester Township. It was here that Garet's second child, Barbara, was born in 1750. His third child, Catherine Elizabeth, was born in 1754,[100] which was also the year that war break out in Pennsylvania. The *French and Indian War* erupted in Pennsylvania in 1754 in Fort Duquesne, near Pittsburgh. Colonists had increasingly been pushing further westward but the French and Indians were preventing

---

[97] Part 1: Pennsylvania Germans: The History Behind Their Focus on Land and Community. February 5, 2022, posted by Heidi Mathis. https://familylocket.com/part-1-pennsylvania-germans-the-history-behind-their-focus-on-land-and-community/
[98] Fogleman, Aaron Spencer. H. *Hopeful Journeys, German Immigration, Settlement, and Political Culture in Colonial America 1717-1775*. (Philadelphia: University of Pennsylvania Press, 1996) Chapter 1.
[99] Ibid
[100] Ancestry.com Family Trees at Mary Magdalena Whittaker Family Tree.

colonial expansion. George Washington, who was fighting with British troops at that time, had failed to persuade the French to leave the Pennsylvania territory. When they refused, Washington gave the order to fire the first shots that started the war.

The war was between Great Britain and France who were fighting for control of the North American continent. The war would last until 1763. Primary battles sites were in Pennsylvania (Fig 27); however, it is unlikely Garet witnessed any skirmishes of the war because Lancaster County was about one hundred and fifty miles away to the east.

Figure 27

Garet resided in Manchester Township, Lancaster County. This was a settlement laid out in 1742 and the entire township had three hundred inhabitants—mostly Quakers and Germans. It was primarily an agricultural community. Garet purchased one hundred and thirty acres sometime prior to 1759.[101] (He retained this land for at least ten years as he was assessed taxes on it in 1769). With that much land, he would have taken up farming. His son, John, was only nine years old in 1754 but most likely was needed to help Garet with farming the land.

Manchester Township was fairly close to Philadelphia. That proximity meant that Garet would have received early news about major political events in the Colonies, including the French and Indian War. To colonial settlers, news primarily came by word of mouth, or through town meetings or church services. Taverns and coffee houses were also popular venues for spreading news, but Garet belonged to the Reformed Church and likely did not frequent these places. Of course, there was also the written word, and one assumes that Garet and son, John aged nine, had learned English by this time to read and write. Pamphlets and newspapers, such as Ben Franklin's *Philadelphia Gazette* were also ways the settlers kept informed.

---

[101] Fiscus, Wayne R. "The Fiscus Family Tree, From Rhineland to America." Found on Ancestry.com, Mark Robinson Family Tree.

Just before Garet and Mary Magdalena moved from Manchester Township, their fourth child, Charles was born in Manchester Township.

By 1760, Garet and Mary Magdalena had relocated to Maytown, Lancaster County, Pennsylvania which was not far from Manchester Township. Figure 28 depicts the remaining colonial vestiges of Maytown today. Their fifth child, Abraham, was born in 1760 in Maytown.

Figure 28

Maytown has a remarkably interesting history. It was officially founded May 1, 1760, and its history is recorded by the *Maytown Historical Society*.[102] A German Mennonite couple, Jacob Downer and his wife, purchased one hundred and fifty acres in Lancaster County and recruited German immigrants.

The Downers selected the site for Maytown to create a frontier community near the Susquehanna River and Great Peter's Road. It was a perfect location as a supply center for immigrants who were moving westward. The Downers invited selected German immigrants and sold them town lots. Garet must have been one of those early recruits, as he is on record as being in Maytown in 1759, one year prior to the town's official incorporation.

The Downers collected annual rental fees on each deeded property. They laid out Maytown so it featured a central diamond-shaped town square with grid pattern streets. There were sixteen blocks subdivided into four lots, creating space for a moderately sized dwelling, a small barn or stable, and a garden although many townspeople owned their own acreages outside of town to raise crops for cash, or feeding livestock, or growing food for their families.

Garet must have been attracted to the well-designed community. He was among the first to move there. Other Germans were relocating to the village and they shared his customs and language. Most importantly, there was the opportunity to own land adjacent to the village. The village quickly secured many businesses

---

[102] Maytown Historical Society. https://maytownhistory.com/history/

Palatine to American Patriot

that could meet the needs of the settlers and make it a more self-sustaining community.

Maytown became a popular resting place for travelers heading west. It is said that the skills of German immigrants in metal, leather, and woodcrafts earned the community a good reputation that drew other artisans. Businesses in colonial Maytown included blacksmiths, hardware stores, taverns, and inns to meet the needs of the travelers as well as those living in the surrounding territories. Garet's skills as a tailor surely made him a valuable asset in Maytown.

The town benefited from trade made possible by its close proximity to the Susquehanna River. Fur trading was an important part of the trade among settlers. One of the most famous fur trappers of the region was a Frenchman named Pierre Bezaillion.[103] He carved out many of the wilderness trails surrounding Maytown that facilitated trade. Even today, the network of narrow and twisty roads carved by Bezaillion can still be seen.

The land around Maytown was used for growing crops, and tobacco was a popular one. In the winter, during the off-season, the residents of Maytown would sustain themselves as cobblers, coopers, and cabinetmakers.[104] So it seems reasonable to assume that Garet would have worked his one hundred and thirty acres during the spring and summer to grow and harvest crops for his family. Then, like others, he would have used the winter months to work as a tailor, including perhaps working with fur pelts that were abundant in the area.

By 1761, Garet was firmly established in Maytown. He was thirty-six and Mary Magdalena was thirty-two. Their children now ranged in age from twenty to one. Their oldest son, John Fiscus, left home on September 11, 1761, and enlisted for duty in the First Company "K" Regiment Infantry under Captain Henry at Kittanning, Pennsylvania. He was mustered into service on October 12 under Captain Hays (Fig 29).[105] Although the French and Indian War was still being waged, most of the fighting had technically ended

---

[103] Welcome to Lancaster County. http://www.welcome-to-lancaster-county.com/maytown.html
[104] Ibid.
[105] https://www.phmc.state.pa.us/bah/dam/rg/di/r19-65RegisterPaVolunteers/r19-65Regt078/r19-65Regt078 pg 115.pdfSon John, age 20, enlists in Compan

in the Colonies by 1760. Thus, John Fiscus' military service at Kittanning, in Armstrong County about 250 miles to the west of Maytown, was focused primarily on deterring Native American campaigns.[106]

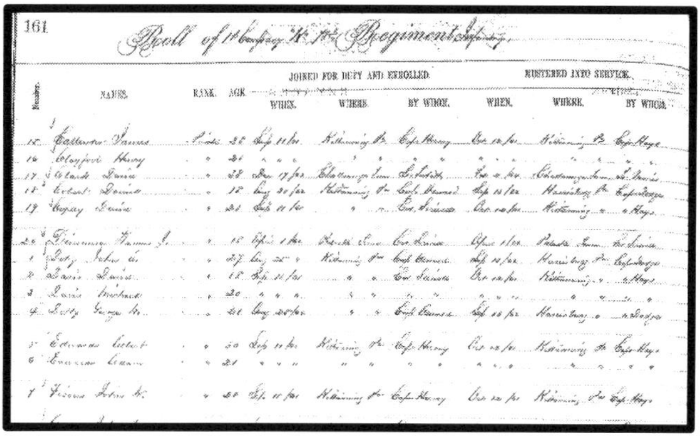
161

Roll of

NAMES. RANK. AGE.

JOINED FOR DUTY AND ENROLLED. WHEN. WHERE. BY WHOM.

MUSTERED INTO SERVICE. WHEN. WHERE. BY WHOM.

Figure 29

PRE-REVOLUTION

In 1763 the *Treaty of Paris* finally ended the French and Indian War. But the nine-year battle left England nearly broke. The Crown imposed new taxes on the American Colonists to refill their coffers. England also faced a significant challenge in maintaining order in the Colonies because relations with the Native American tribes was not good following the French and Indian war. So the British kept a standing army in America, and that led to a variety of problems with their Colonists—especially in Pennsylvania. An uprising on the Ohio frontier, *Pontiac's Rebellion*, led to the *Proclamation of 1763*, which forbade colonial settlement west of the Allegany Mountains. This was viewed as particularly egregious to land-hungry Pennsylvania settlers and land speculators, like George Washington.[107]

Britain was starting to sow seeds of discontent.

---

[106] https://en.wikipedia.org/wiki/Kittanning_(village)

[107] Library of Congress. https://www.loc.gov/classroom-materials/united-states-history-primary-source-timeline/american-revolution-1763-1783/british-reforms-1763-1766/

In 1765, England passed the *Stamp Act*. Its purpose was to replenish at least half of the costs of Britain's wartime defenses from the French and Indian War. Again, England looked to its American Colonies as a revenue source. Almost immediately, *The Stamp Act* was wildly unpopular. The Colonists, especially in Philadelphia, which was only seventy miles from Maytown where Garet lived, rebelled against this new tax on all paper documents. Indeed, Philadelphia became a major site of colonists' rebellion. Pennsylvania colonists argued that only their own representative assemblies could tax them. They saw the Act as unconstitutional. In Philadelphia, there was mob violence designed to intimidate stamp collectors into resigning.

It was amid this colonial turmoil that John Fiscus married Catherine Fans on December 15, 1766. They were wed by Reverend John Conrad Bucher in Cumberland County, about twenty-seven miles from Maytown. In this same year, England repealed *The Stamp Act*, but they issued a *Declaratory Act* at the same time to reaffirm British authority to pass any colonial legislation it saw fit.[108] Adding fuel to the fire, England passed the *Townsend Acts* just one year later in 1767. This forced the incorrigible Colonists to comply with British demands. It was particularly outrageous to Pennsylvanians who had long prized their self-government. William Penn had always allowed Colonists in his province to govern themselves.

The Province of Pennsylvania was now simmering in bitter discontent against the British. The British had grossly underestimated the independent spirit of their American Colonists.

THE GERMAN REFORMED CHURCH IN AMERICA

For most German immigrants, religion was central to their lives. During the eighteenth century, the British American Colonies were overwhelmingly Protestant. It is estimated there were only 25,000 Catholics out of 4.5 million in the Colonies at the time of independence in 1776.[109] This is not surprising since the British had

---

[108] The Stamp Act. https://www.history.com/topics/american-revolution/stamp-act
[109] Roman Catholicism in America. https://www.britannica.com/topic/Roman-Catholicism/Roman-Catholicism-in-the-United-States-and-Canada

heavily promoted Protestant immigration. In general, the British American Colonies did not welcome Catholics and, indeed, many Colonies even excluded Catholics whereas Congregational or Episcopal churches were supported by law.[110] Pennsylvania was the only Colony that tolerated Catholicism and allowed mass to be celebrated in public. In fact, there was no other Colony that began with as many religious denominations and as much genuine religious toleration as Pennsylvania.[111]

The German Protestants in Pennsylvania had all sprung from the sixteenth century Reformation. They constituted two distinct branches: German Reformed and Lutheran Churches. The largest of these was the German Reformed, later just referred to as the Reformed Church. Garet came to the Colonies as a member of the Reformed Church and he remained so until he died. His children were all active in the Reformed Church and later would help found other such churches in Pennsylvania.

Both the Reformed Churches and the Lutheran Churches were kept up almost entirely by the German speaking immigrants bound by lineage, language, and the same liturgies. Both congregations frequently worshipped in the same church or schoolhouse. Both churches had democratic forms of governance, wherein the minister and certain elected representatives from the congregation governed the church.[112]

In eighteenth century Pennsylvania, there was a shortage of pastors so the nearest pastor of either church was asked to baptize, perform a marriage ceremony, or read the last rites of the dead. Church services for both groups were held at the house of some German Reformed or Lutheran family and reading from the Bible and the offering prayers came from a German prayer book. A schoolmaster conducted catechism classes for the children. By cooperating, the Lutheran and Reformed Churches were able to hold their people together till they could afford their own church and preacher.

---

[110] Ibid
[111] History of Westmoreland County, Volume 1, Chapter 22. https://www.pa-roots.com/westmoreland/historyproject/vol1/chap22.html
[112] History of Westmoreland County. Vol 1, Ch 22. The Churches.. https://www.pa-roots.com/westmoreland/historyproject/vol1/chap22.html

The Reformed and the Lutheran Churches owned nearly all their church property in common. They worshiped alternately in these churches, and quite often their ministers' performed services for each other. Members of these churches intermarried more than in other churches and were buried finally side by side in the common graveyard. Church members would eventually secure land and erect a log church as quickly as they were able. They would also build a small house for the pastor and a schoolhouse near the church. The pastor's house always had some extra land attached, so that he could have a garden for subsistence. There would be a cemetery nearby.[113,114]

Garet Fiscus and his family were actively involved in the Reformed Church and it surely played a major role in their lives, even shaping their political views favoring American independence as we shall see later. In 1765, Garet was elected trustee of the Maytown Reformed Church,[115] (which still thrives as the *Maytown Reformed United Church of Christ*).[116] For the first five years, preaching services were held in private homes and services were held by various itinerant pastors. The earliest recorded pastor at the Maytown Reformed church was Reverend John Conrad Bucher, who had performed the marriage service for Garet's son John to Catherine Fans. In 1766, Garet and Mary Magdalena had their sixth child, Magdalena (1766 – 1797). Garet was now forty-one years old and Mary Magdalena was thirty-seven. All of their children were baptized in the Reformed Church. In 1766, their children were John, twenty-one; Barbara, ten; Catherine, eleven; Charles, seven; and Abraham six.

On August 1, 1769, Garet and another church trustee, Christian Fox, purchased two lots on Elizabeth Street in Maytown from Jacob Downer and his wife (both of whom had laid out the town of Maytown).[117] The original deed for the property is held in the archives

---

[113] Ibid.
[114] Westmoreland County Historical Project. Vol 1, Ch 22. https://www.pa-roots.com/westmoreland/historyproject/vol1/chap22.html
[115] Notes from Elma Fiscus 1975 letter to Mary Smith.
[116] Maytown Reformed United Church of Christ History. https://maytownreformeducc.com/church-history/
[117] Ibid.
[73.] Ibid.

of the Hague in Holland.[118] That same year, Garet oversaw the construction of a log building to house the church. It was the first Reformed Church in Donegal Township. The log structure served as the sanctuary until 1805.

The collective attitude of the German Reformed settlers in Maytown was exemplary of other Pennsylvania Dutch settlers. They possessed a spirit of independence and mutual support that surely prepared them well for their part in the Revolution to come.

But Garet was not yet content.

His eyes were turned westward toward the new county of Westmoreland where there was a wide open frontier and the opportunity to own more of his own land.

---

[118] Ibid

CHAPTER EIGHT

Westmoreland County 1769 - 1797

Westmoreland County was the last new county in Pennsylvania created before the Revolution. It had the distinction of being the first county located entirely west of the Allegheny Mountains.[119]

The land for Westmoreland County had been purchased by the family of William Penn from the Six Nations or Iroquois Indians in November 1768, and it was opened for settlement the following April 1769.[120] When Westmoreland was settled it covered broadly what was known as Southwestern Pennsylvania, the total area being about four thousand and seven hundred square miles.

---

[119] https://www.phmc.state.pa.us/portal/communities/pa-history/1681-1776.html
[120] Westmoreland County Pennsylvania Genealogy Project at: https://www.pa-roots.com/westmoreland/oldwestmoreland/chapter01.html

The Forbes Road, known as *The Great Road to the West*, was a major route westward in Pennsylvania. It was a military road built in 1755 as a major migration route in the French and Indian War. There were tavern keepers along Forbes Road that provided shelter and entertainment to persons traveling on it and doing the King's business. By 1769, Forbes Road had become a major migration route for Pennsylvania settlers heading west. It was the first improved road to cross the barrier of the successive ridgelines of the Appalachian Mountains.[121]

In 1769, Garet traveled the Forbes Road to move his family to Westmoreland County. He was taking them to an area of Pennsylvania that was described as "...*trackless forest, peopled with hostile Indians, and fraught with dangers from wild beasts...*"[122]

Garet would have traveled across Pennsylvania in a Conestoga wagon (Fig 30), which was used exclusively in the United States from the early eighteenth to mid-nineteenth centuries. It was a heavy and large horse-drawn vehicle which originated most likely from German immigrants of Pennsylvanian Dutch culture in the province of Pennsylvania in the early eighteenth century.[123] The trip from Maytown to Westmoreland County was about one hundred and eighty miles. A two-horse drawn Conestoga wagon could cover from fifteen to twenty miles per day, after which the horses required water, food, and rest.

Figure 30

With six children, the journey probably took two weeks.

---

[121] Ibid.
[122] Western Pennsylvania Historical Magazine, Vol 7, No 3. July 1924.p. 151
[123] Conestoga Wagons. https://www.history.com/topics/19th-century/conestoga-wagon

LAND OWNERSHIP

As soon as they were able, immigrants wanted to purchase land. Many, like Garet, had come from land-starved Europe where remnants of the feudal system made it impossible to own land. Garet had purchased his first property, one hundred and thirty acres, in Lancaster County in 1759. He held onto it until at least 1769 when he was assessed taxes on it.

Now he wanted to own land in Westmoreland County.

The process of purchasing land in the Province of Pennsylvania in 1769 was a complicated one. First, the prospective landowner had to file an application for land in fairly specific terms. When the Land Office received the application, they issued a warrant, or an order to have the desired tract surveyed. The applicant had to pay a fee for this warrant and became known as the warrantee. The loose warrant was copied into a ledger called a Warrant Register.

The second step to owning land was to pay a fee for the survey and wait until a deputy surveyor could be assigned to do the work. The results of the survey were returned to the Land Office with a precise description and map of the tract, nearly always including the names of the neighbors who owned the adjacent tracts.

The last step was to pay a fee to the Province of Pennsylvania and receive the final title which was called a patent. This was the official deed transferring ownership from the colony to the individual. He or she now became the patentee. The patents were copied into ledgers called Patent Registers. Sometimes, many years passed between the three steps.[124]

THE FISCUS "PLANTATION"

Garet, age forty-four, submitted three applications for purchase of land in Mount Pleasant, Unity Township, Westmoreland County, Pennsylvania on April 11, 1769. They were for nine hundred acres total: three hundred acres each for himself and for his sons Abraham

---

[124] Original Warrant Registers of PA: All Counties.
https://ancestortracks.com/warrant_registers_CD.htm

Fiscus (age nine) and Charles Fiscus (age ten). Garet was setting his young sons up for the future by titling the land in their names. His oldest son, John, was twenty-four years old, married and still serving in the Infantry. John bought his own three hundred acres on July 20, 1769. John's land was contiguous to Garet's. This brought the total plot size of Fiscus property to twelve hundred acres…a virtual plantation, indeed. Garet's land was contiguous with the ancestors of General John J. Pershing.[125]

Original documents for his land application, surveys, and deeds are displayed in the following figures.

GARET'S ORIGINAL 1769 LAND APPLICATIONS

---

[125] Sons of American Revolution application Jesse Albers 1970.

GARET'S ORIGINAL 1769 LAND DESCRIPTIONS[126]

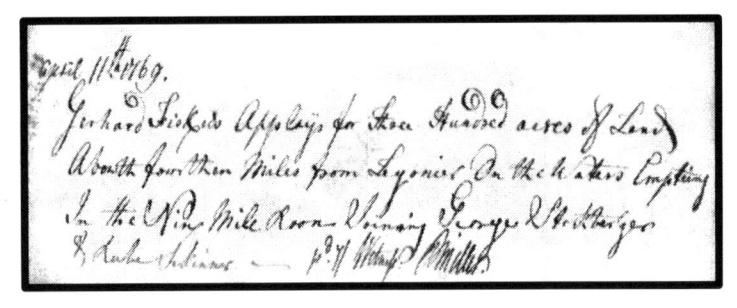

Transcription: *"Gerhart Fiskes applies for land about fourteen miles from Legonier on the waters emptying in the Nine Mile join'g Geo. Stockberger & Rube Sckinner"*

Transcription: *"Charles Fiscus applies for land on the waters emptying in ye 9 mile Run join'g Jerhard Fiscus & Sam'l Hook."*

Transcription *"Abraham Fiscus applies for land about 15 miles from Legonier on the waters emptying into Sewickley join'g Sam'l. Hook Jun'r."*

---

[126] Pennsylvania, U.S., Land Warrants, 1733-1987 Recorded deed

Transcription: *"John Fiscus applies for A Location of a Piece of Land of three hundred acres adjoing to the Nine Mile Runn and joing to Land of Gerhart Fiscus where his Springwaters run in the Ruhn for John Fiscus."*

GARET'S ORIGINAL 1769 SURVEYS OF LAND[127]

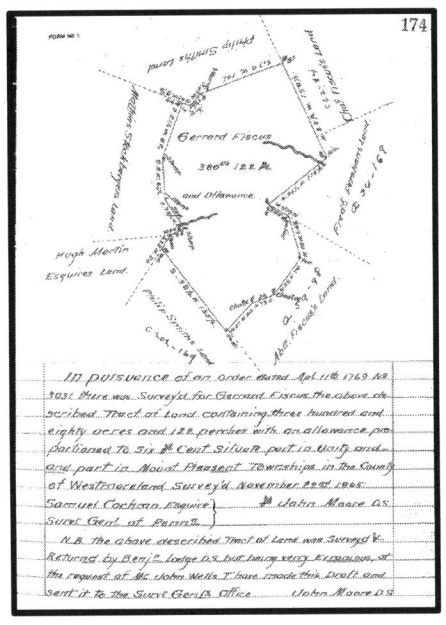

Garet Fiscus Survey   *John Fiscus Survey*

No doubt one of the first things Garet did after completing his land purchase in 1769 was to construct a log cabin home for his family, if only temporarily until he could construct a larger and more permanent home of brick. A brick home was a sign of stability and the owner's "position." To build his log cabin home would have been no small task. It would have required clearing trees, sawing, and splitting about fifty logs, and collecting large stones for the foundation, fireplace, and hearth. His sons Charles, eleven, and Abraham, ten would have helped him. Figure 31 depicts a rudimentary cabin in Pennsylvania estimated to have been built around this time in 1770.

Figure 31

---

[127] The Warrant Register notes that Gerhart's land was "ret'd & ca 24th April 1807 to JnoWills on Wt." Charles land was "Retd &ca 17 Novem'r 1820 to J Fiscus & H. Furry in trust &c on Wt." and Abraham Fiscus land was "10 as. Retd & ca 11th Febry 1823 to A. Fiscus."

In 1771, Garet's seventh child, Mary, was born. Garet was fifty-one years old and Mary Magdalena was forty-seven. The pre-revolutionary activities were gearing up in full force at this time. Colonial resentment toward the British was running high, and especially so for Garet who would experience the oppression of British rule in a very personal way…ejectionment.

EJECTIONMENT

In 1773, the British filed a suit against Charles Fiscus (only fourteen years old) to seize the land Garet had purchased for him. The legal action was known as Ejectionment. In British ejectionment cases, a fictional name was often used against the property owner. Here is how they filed their case against Charles.

> *"No. 161. William Ferguson versus Charles Fiscus, tenant. Ejectment."* [128]

The British practice of ejectionment in eighteenth-century North American Colonies was a well-known practice, and its purpose was to retitle the desired piece of land by means of a variety of actions, including ejectment. For historical reasons, the English action of ejectment was framed in the form of a claim by a lessee of the land that he or she had been ejected from the land. By the eighteenth-century, the lease in many but not all cases, was fictional as was the lessee.[129]

The case brought against Charles was won or at least dismissed because Charles retained his land as evidenced in later tax documents.

---

[128] Source: Minute Book A, Westmoreland County Court Records, Westmoreland Co.,Pa., July Term, 1773. p. 19. http://www.pa-roots.org/data/read.php?840,610036,610036#msg-610036
[129] Harvard University at https://amesfoundation.law.harvard.edu/ColonialAppeals/ejectment.php

FIRST GRAND JURY INQUEST

The newly formed county of Westmoreland required a judicial system. To constitute a new County Court, the Pennsylvania governor named twenty-six persons living in Westmoreland County to be Justices of the Peace and Justices of the County Court—any three of whom could adjudicate cases. This would be the first and only court west of the Alleghenies to administer English Common Law under His Majesty, the King of England. Thus, any cases brought before the new Westmoreland County Court were always worded, *"The King vs.[John Doe]."*

The location of the Westmoreland County Court was Robert Hanna's home (a re-creation of the home appears in Figure 32). Hanna's house was about three miles from Garet's property. Robert Hanna's house was well known in those days because it was near Forbes Road. A tavern Mr. Hanna had constructed nearby was also well-known. Its signage read, *"Entertainment for Man and Beast."*[130]

Figure 32

Jurisdiction of the Westmoreland County Court at Hanna's house would extend from 1773 until the close of the American Revolution in April of 1783.[131] The very first trial in Westmoreland, referred to as the *"First Grand Inquest"* was held on April 6, 1773. Garet ("Garrett Fickes" sic) (Fig 33)[132] was one of fifteen jurors appointed to serve. Garet would serve as juror for the next ten years.

Figure 33

Garet's appointment to the Court tells us that he had some standing in the community, and that his reputation was one of integrity. It also tells us that he had learned to speak English well enough to be seated with fourteen other jurors mostly likely of Irish

---
[130] Western Pennsylvania Historical Magazine, https://journals.psu.edu/wph/article/view/1353/1201
[131] Sons of American Revolution application of Jesse Aber, January 1970.
[132] Western Pennsylvania Historical Magazine. Vol 7, No. 3. Pp. 9-10

and English heritage. When he had lived in Maytown, populated with mostly German immigrants, he could still speak in his native tongue. However, when he moved to the frontier of Westmoreland County, he would have required an ability to speak fluent English in order to survive. Thus, Garet must have made a concerted effort to assimilate in his new country and early on, as opposed other immigrant groups that saw themselves as "foreigners" in a new country. Garet saw himself as an American.

At the very first session of the *Grand Inquest*, there were four trials heard. Since the court was administered under British Common Law, the cases typically read as "The King" versus the accused. The following is the first case that Garet heard:

The King	*Forcible entry, true Bill Deft,*
vs	*being three times solemnly*
Garett Pendergrass	*called appears not (process awarded Curr) process is dismissed*[133]

Even though Westmoreland County was on the western frontier, they were not immune to pre-revolution political events. Indeed, as tensions grew between England and the Colonies in the 1770s, the settlers in Westmoreland County also felt rebellious. In fact, so rebellious that several officials of the Court met at the Courthouse in Hannastown in May 1775 and passed the *Westmoreland Resolves*. It was an early expression of American rights. It read:

> *"it had therefore become the indisputable duty of every American, of any man who had any public virtue or love for his country, or any compassion for posterity, to resist and oppose by every means which God had put in his power the*

---

[133] Ibid.

execution of this system, and that as for them they would be ready to oppose it with their lives and fortunes"[134]

BARBARA FISCUS MCCULLOUGH MURDER

Little is known about Garet's second child, Barbara. She married William McCullough (or McColloch) (1749 – 1831) and they had a son John in 1770. They may have had other children but we do not know for certain. Garet's last will and testament in 1797 referred to his grandson, John, as the *"only surviving child"* of Barbara, which seems to imply other children, but perhaps not.

According to an 1895 book entitled *"Butler County History"* Barbara died in 1774. The book claims she was murdered by a hired hand. However, a 1912 article in the *'Butler Citizen'* newspaper states that Barbara was actually killed in an Indian massacre.

Garet and Mary Magdalena took in Barbara's son, John McCullough, to raise. When Garet died in 1797, he included grandson John McCullough, twenty-seven years old at that time, in his will. John McCullough grew to become a Captain in the military and achieve his own success in life.

AMERICAN REVOLUTION 1775

The first shots of the Revolutionary War were fired in Lexington, Massachusetts in 1775. Garet was fifty-one and his son John was thirty-one, Charles seventeen, and Abraham sixteen years. Philadelphia was the central location for Revolutionary War activity and it was only about one hundred and eighty miles away from the Fiscus homes in Westmoreland County.

In 1775, the Second Congress in Philadelphia immediately busied itself in raising militias, directing strategies for the rebellion, and appointing diplomats. On July 2, 1776, the Continental Congress

---

[134] War on the Pennsylvania Frontier.

declared independence from Britain. Two days later they unanimously agreed to the Declaration of Independence.

But long before independence was declared in Philadelphia, the American Colonists had already begun aligning their allegiances. Some of the pacifist German groups in Pennsylvania, like the Quakers, remained neutral. Others remained loyal to England, including the extended family members of William Penn who still governed Pennsylvania. The Penns were Tories or British Loyalists.

Garet and his family were avowed Patriots. The Continental Union Flag (Fig 34) was the flag of the United Colonies from 1775 to 1776, and the de facto flag of the United States until 1777, when the thirteen star flag was adopted by the Continental Congress. The Continental Union flag was flown in Westmoreland County, which had become openly rebellious against England.

Figure 34

What factors persuaded Garet and his sons to become Patriots against England?

First, they were greatly influenced by their German Reformed Church. The German Reformed Church openly supported independence from the British from the onset of the pre-revolutionary events and throughout the American Revolution. In fact, a German Reformed pastor, Caspar Weyberg, spoke openly in favor of independence during the British occupation of Philadelphia.[135] One author writes:

> "...during the American Revolution both [German Reformed] pastors and people were ardent supporters of the independence movement and were almost without exception loyal to the patriot cause."[136]

---

[135] Donald E. Harpster.Pennsylvania History: A Journal of Mid-Atlantic Studies (2023) 90 (1): 1–34.https://doi.org/10.5325/pennhistory.90.1.0001
[136]Weaver, G. The German Reformed Church and Civil Government 1775 – 1855. file:///C:/Users/mecra/Downloads/mlb78,+phj194910v16i4p03 (2).pdf

Palatine to American Patriot

The German Reformed immigrants had always been clannish and settled in their own communities. They often continued to speak German, including at their church services, and they still adhered to their European theological and liturgical heritage embodied in the Heidelberg Catechism and the Palatinate Liturgy.[137] But at the onset of pre-Revolutionary events and certainly by the outbreak of the American Revolution, German Reformed Church members in Pennsylvania quickly began to assimilate as "Americans." That is, they no longer viewed themselves as "foreigners" living in America. They had begun to identify with their new country. When American independence was threatened, the German Reformed Church had no qualms in openly promoting American independence among its members and at church services. The pastors encouraged support of the American Patriots. It was also the start of the German Reformed Churches beginning to use English in their services.

The second influencing factor for Garet and his family to become Patriots is that Westmoreland County became a well-known center of Revolutionary rebellion. It was filled with highly independent-minded settlers who owned land. They had a vested interest in America and they no longer wanted to live under the threat of property seizure by the British.

Westmoreland County was also a significant site for Patriot militia activity. Residents formed battalions to support the Continental Army's fight for independence. Hannastown, located near Garet's property, was a rallying point for local militia and a center for revolutionary sentiment. The people of Westmoreland County immediately passed resolutions to resist British rule. Indeed, before most other Colonial communities took a stand against British oppression, Westmoreland County residents proclaimed their willingness to take up arms to defend their rights against Great Britain and support the besieged residents of Boston.

The *Hannastown Resolves* were one of the most direct challenges to British authority in their North American Colonies preceding the Declaration of Independence and the American Revolutionary War. Before most other Colonial communities took a

---
[137] Ibid.

stand, Westmoreland County, Pennsylvania residents proclaimed their willingness to take drastic measures to maintain and defend their rights against British oppression. The *Hannastown Resolves* declared the establishment of a local militia.[138] Garet was still a juror of the *Grand Inquest Westmoreland County Court*. They continued to meet in the Hannastown Courthouse, so he would have been party to the *Resolves*.

The *Independent Batallion of Westmoreland County Pennsylvania*, led by the sheriff of Hannastown, was among the first American troops west of the Alleghenies. They served in conflicts in the East and Western frontier borders from 1775 to 1781, and later until 1795. Hannastown served as a recruitment center for the county militia and Continental Army. Their flag, featuring a rattlesnake ready to strike the British Union Jack and the words "*Don't Tread on Me*," is still the official flag of Westmoreland County.[139]

When the American Revolution erupted, Garet had been farming his land in Westmoreland County for about six years. It should be remembered that in 1775, besides the Revolutionary activities that were going on, there were also high tensions between settlers and Native Americans. Westmoreland County was still a frontier area. Settlers, feeling threatened, had formed militias to defend against the Indians. The settlers faced increasing challenges from Indian attacks and internal strife. The Native American tribes, including the Seneca, were often seen as enemies due to conflicts over land and resources. Garet's own daughter, Barbara, had been murdered by Indians the previous year of 1774. Thus, Garet and his family needed to deal with a double threat in Westmoreland County: the American Revolution and defending Indian attacks on their person and property.

> "*the Indians [in Westmoreland County] remained quiet during 1775 and the following winter, but it was not long until the agents of the British government outbid the colonists for a savage alliance. The British were able to give them greater bribes and to impress the savages with great*

---

[138] https://en.wikipedia.org/wiki/Hanna%27s_town_resolves
[139] Westmoreland Historical Society. https://westmorelandhistory.org/hannas-town/

displays of military force…the Iroquois accepted the war hatchet and to fight for the king."[140]

The settlers in Westmoreland County anticipated the Indian threat and they raised a company of young riflemen who patrolled along the Allegheny River.[141] Life was precarious for Garet and his family. But they stood their ground. Indeed, the Fiscus men actually ran toward danger…they enlisted in the militia for the American Revolution.

AMERICAN REVOLUTION OATH OF FIDELITY

At the outbreak of the hostilities in 1775, the Pennsylvania Assembly opposed any form of mandatory military service. So activist elements in Pennsylvania organized local volunteer "associations" that were eventually formed into fifty-three battalions. It wasn't until 1777 that the Assembly passed Pennsylvania's first militia law requiring compulsory military service of all able-bodied male whites between the ages of eighteen and fifty-three. Exemptions were extremely limited, and an estimated sixty thousand men were enrolled.

On February 3, 1778, the Continental Congress passed a resolution that read:

> *"Resolved, That all officers of the army shall take and subscribe the foregoing oath or affirmation before the commander in chief, or any major general or brigadier general" (JCC, X, 11)* [142]

The following Oath of Allegiance was tendered to white males over eighteen in Pennsylvania:

---

[140] American Archives, Fourth series, vol vi, p. 764; fifth series, vol 1, p. 867.
[141] Ibid.
[142] https://www.phmc.state.pa.us/bah/dam/rg/di/RevolutionaryWarPensionersIndex/RevolutionaryWarPensionersIndex_F.htm

"I, ----------, do swear (or affirm) that I renounce and refuse all allegiance to George the Third, King of Great Britain, his heirs and successors, and that I will be faithful and bear true allegiance to the commonwealth of Pennsylvania as a free and independent state, and that I will not at any time do or cause to be done any matter or thing that will be prejudicial or injurious to the freedom and independence thereof, as declared by Congress; and also that I will discover and make known to some one justice of the peace of the said state all treasons 2 and traitorous conspiracies which I now know or hereafter shall know to be formed against this or any of the United States of America."[Pa3 111-112] This oath has three elements that were common in many of the oaths during the Revolution. It includes an abjuration of allegiance to the King of England; it includes promise of allegiance to the state as an independent state; and, it includes a commitment to reveal treasons and conspiracies against any of the states. Every state required some promise of allegiance. This usually took the form of a promise of allegiance to his particular state, sometimes as a free and independent state, or in some cases, to the United States as free and independent states. Massachusetts and Rhode Island did not mention allegiance to the State, but required a man to pledge that he supported the war opposing Great Britain [Ma1 479, RI1 1

AMERICAN REVOLUTIONARY PATRIOTS

Figure 35

On June 10, 1777, Charles Fiscus, eighteen years old, enlisted in the Second Company of the Second Battalion of the Westmoreland County Militia as an ensign. His neighbor, Hugh Martin, was captain of the battalion. Transcription of his enlistment is found in Fig 35.[143]

In 1783 John Fiscus is listed as a Private on the Roster of Company I, 168th Pennsylvania Regiment. His date of enlistment is not known, but it could have been continuous from when he first enlisted in 1761.

Abraham Fiscus also served in the militia. His enlistment date is not known, but his service is documented through the *Pennsylvania, U.S., Tax Exoneration 1768 – 1801*[144], which the Sons of the American Revolution (SAR) and Daughters of the American Revolution (DAR) recognize as official proof of Patriotic military service.[145] The *Tax and Exoneration Lists* (Fig 36 and 37) identify individuals exempted from taxes due to their support for the Revolutionary War effort, perhaps due to their political

Figure 36

---

[143] Pennsylvania, U.S., Veterans Card Files, 1775-1916 for Charles Fiskey **Revolutionary War Military Abstract Card File**
[144] Pennsylvania, U.S., Tax and Exoneration, 1768-1801 for Westmoreland County.
[145] Evaluation of Tax and Exoneration Lists in the Pennsylvania State Archives as a Basis for Patriot Service. 2013. https://members.sar.org/media/uploads/pages/228/kdupnXMF0xEw.pdf

status or participation in the war itself. Garet and his three sons appear on the Exoneration Lists in two different years.

Abraham Fiscus' Revolutionary War service is further documented based on his name appearing on the *Revolutionary War Pension List*. In later years, his widow Catherine received Revolutionary War pension monies.

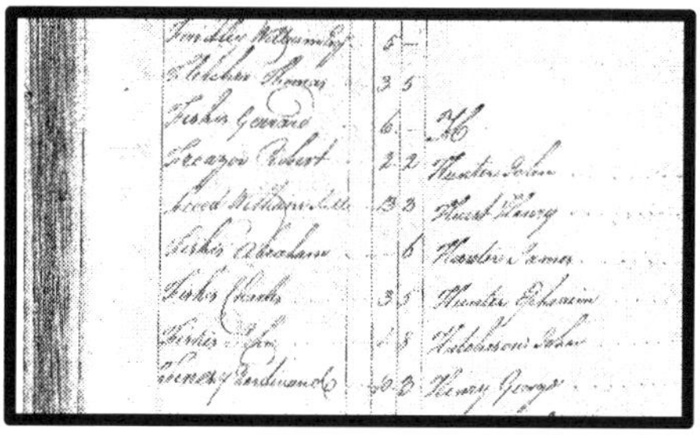

Figure 37

On June 19, 1778, Garet signed the Oath of Allegiance in support of American independence. John Fiscus signed the Oath on May 23, 1778, as a requirement of his military service.[146] Charles Fiscus and Abraham Fiscus also served in the military and would have signed the Oath as part of their military enlistment.

---

[146] Pennsylvania Archives Series 3, Vol III, page 32.

CHAPTER NINE

Post Revolution 1781 - 1790

In 1781, the British army surrendered at Yorktown. The Revolutionary War was essentially over after that, except that the British still held New York City and Charleston, S.C. In January of 1782, over one hundred thousand Loyalists in America could see the hand-writing on the wall. They departed for Canada, England, or Europe. Of those Loyalists who remained, most lost what they had, including the Penns.

AMBUSH OF HANNASTOWN

One of the final actions of the American Revolution occurred on July 13, 1782, in Hannastown, Westmoreland County, Pennsylvania (Fig 38). Hannastown was less than three miles from Garet's family farms.

Sayenqueraghta, a war chief of the eastern Seneca tribe along with three hundred warriors dressed in castoff uniforms

Figure 38

from the King's Eighth Regiment, and about thirty British soldiers attacked and destroyed Hannastown. Hannastown had been the county seat with more than thirty log cabins, three taverns and a courthouse (where Garet was still serving as an appointed Juror for trials). The attack on Hannastown was the biggest attack that occurred during the Revolutionary War in western Pennsylvania. It is thought that Hannastown was a target because it was the only true example of colonial civilian government in the western Pennsylvania frontier. After the attack, only two buildings were left standing, one of them being the fort surrounding Hannastown. Letters that were written in the days after the ambush talk about the capture of Robert Hanna, and the suffering of the residents who had nothing left but the clothes on their backs. Two of the town's residents were killed.[147]

The attack disrupted the political system of western Pennsylvania because of the destruction of the Courthouse. Hannastown reverted to farmland, and Westmoreland County's seat moved to Greensburg in 1786. Newspaper accounts from that time tell how deeply the attack on Hannastown had impacted nearby settlers' lives, including Garet and his family. For many years thereafter, locals held memorial services at the site.[148]

On September 3, 1783, a peace treaty was reached in Paris and it was official…the Revolutionary War was finally over. America was an independent nation. The American Patriots had carried the day. Garet was now fifty-eight years old and Mary Magdalena was fifty-four. Their sons' military service was ended and they could continue with their lives in a free America. Garet had provided farmland for his sons and that became their occupation. The Indian skirmishes had largely ceased after the Revolutionary War as the Indians were pushed further west. Their alliance with the British during the Revolution did nothing to advance their cause.

---

[147] https://www.southcoasttoday.com/story/news/nation-world/2007/09/23/225-years-later-anthropologist-reveals/52787605007/. Attack on Hannastown, PA
[148] History of Westmoreland County, Vol 2, Ch 1. https://www.pa-roots.com/westmoreland/historyproject/vol1/chap11.html

MOUNT PLEASANT TOWNSHIP

In 1783, documents show Garet's address was Mount Pleasant Township, Westmoreland County, Pennsylvania---very near his farmland. This change in address was not a physical move, but rather a redistricting of Westmoreland County.

Mount Pleasant Township was founded on April 6, 1773, as one of the eleven original townships of the newly created Westmoreland County. It was occupied, at the time of founding, by roving Indian bands with temporary villages and camps, but no permanent villages. Like Garet, the first settlers were mostly young men of German descent. They would first clear their lands and built log houses. Farming was the principal occupation, as it was for Garet. It is said that the rich limestone clay soil in Westmoreland County raised good crops, chiefly grains. Later, large brick houses were built as a symbol of permanency.[149]

In 1782, not long after the Hannastown ambush, Garet helped found St. Paul's Reformed (Lutheran) church in Mount Pleasant Township (the reader will recall that the Reformed and Lutheran congregants often shared church buildings). Garet was church trustee of the Reformed Church and he is credited in the church's history as being the one who brought the pastor, Rev. John William Weber, to the church in 1782.[150] Rev. Weber remained the church pastor until his death.

THE FIRST US CENSUS OF 1790

In 1790, George Washington was President and John Adams the Vice-President. Thomas Jefferson was Secretary of State and he directed the first United States Census recorded on August 2, 1790, and as mandated by the new Constitution. It was conducted by marshals who collected data in all thirteen states. Of particular interest was the number of white males under sixteen years, which

---

[149] http://www.mtpleasanttwp.com/history.html
[150] History of the County of Westmoreland with Biographical Sketches of Many of Its Pioneers and Prominent Men. https://babel.hathitrust.org/cgi/pt?id=pst.000046292940&seq=11&q1=Fiscus

was used to assess the industrial and military potential of the United States. The census information was recorded as follows: *"1) free white males under 16 years, 2) free white males 16 years and older 3) free white females, and 4) slaves.*[151]

The total population of the United States in 1790 was 3.9 million people. Pennsylvania's total population was 434,373, which made it the second largest state behind Virginia.

The 1790 U.S. Census identified Garet, John, Abraham, and Charles Fiscus as heads of their own households. They all resided in Unity Township, Westmoreland County, Pennsylvania. (Note: Unity Township was formed in 1789 from Mt. Pleasant Township). Figure 39 depicts the original image of the 1790 Census for Pennsylvania and what was recorded for the Fiscus family heads of

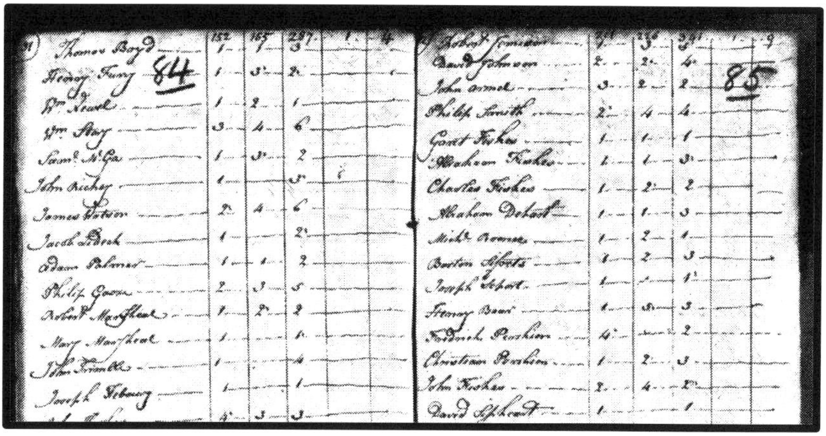

Figure 39

households (note: the spelling was *Fiskes* by the census taker).

Garet "Fiskes" (*sic*) had three total persons in his household: "1 free white male over 16; 1 free white male under sixteen; and 1 free white female." The male youth living with them was the orphaned

---

[151] Pennsylvania's Gradual Abolition Act of 1780 only provided freedom for children born to slaves after its enactment. These children labored for their mothers' masters for twenty-eight years and therefore, in effect, paid slaveholders the cost of their own freedom.

grandson, John McCullough, whose mother Barbara had been murdered.[152]

John "Fiskes" (*sic*) had eight total persons in his household: "2 white males over 16; 4 free white males under 16; and 2 free white females." Besides John and Catharina, which included nine year old son Abraham (1781 – 1850); six year old son Jacob (1784 - ?); and three year old son Wilhelm (1787 - ?). It is unclear who the unaccounted household members are (i.e., one unidentified adult male; one unidentified female; an unidentified male youth). Perhaps these were farm workers living with them.

Charles "Fiskes" (*sic*) had a total of five household members: " 1 free white male over 16, 2 free white males under 16, and 2 free white females." In addition to Garet and his wife Zeruia (Selena in Americanized version), the persons under 16 years would have included his son Jacob age 12 (Charles' illegitimate son); six year old son, David (1784 – 1870) [153]; and one year old daughter, Sara (1789 - ?).

In family lore, Charles was somewhat of a "black sheep" because he had an illegitimate child in 1778 before he married Zeruia in 1780.[154] That illegitimate child was Jacob Fiscus. Church records document the following.

> *"a child was born to Carl Fisgus (illeg) and Elisabeth Barbara on April 3, 1778. He was baptized by a schoolmaster, Baltasar Meyer*[155]*, on May 17, 1778 with Jacob and Catharina Bernhard as his sponsors."*

Elisabeth Barbara was Jacob's mother and her parents were Jacob and Catharina Bernhard. Documents exist showing the Bernhards resided in Pennsylvania and were connected to St. Paul's Lutheran Church. Charles did not marry Elisabeth Barbara, but he

---

[152] Notes from J.A. and Elma Fiscus. Available from Mary Whittaker Family Tree in Ancestry.com
[153] David Fiscus was my 4th great grandfather.
[154] Owens County Cousins. Documentavailable on Ancestry.com Mary Whittaker Family Tree.
[155] It was a known practice to have a schoolmaster perform church events like marriage or birth when a pastor had not yet been secured for a German Reformed church on the frontier.

did give Jacob his name of Fiscus. Charles apparently took Jacob into his household with his wife Zeruia.

Abraham "Fiskes" *(sic)* had five persons living in this household: "1 free white male under 16; 1 free white male under 16; and 3 free white females." Besides him and his wife, Catherine Aukerman (1767 – 1845) that would include: five year old son William Fiscus (1785–1870); two year old daughter Polly Fiscus (1788–); and infant Magdalena Fiscus (abt 1789).

GARET'S DEATH

According to records, on June 18, 1790, Garet Fiscus agreed to sell to his youngest son, Abraham Fiscus and Adam Weaver (his son-in-law) his "plantation" in Unity Township, Westmoreland County, for annual payments of grain and animals until Garrett died.[156] In 1794, family records state that Garet once again sold more of his land.[157] It may have been that Garet had already developed health problems and could no longer tend to his property.

Just three years later, in September of 1797 Garet composed his will. He was severely ailing and states so in his will. Too sick to write it himself, he had a friend transcribe his wishes. He refers to himself as Gerhart, his given German name. His will reflects his strong faith and the ever present sense of responsibility he felt for his family's welfare.

On November 1797, Garet died at age seventy-two in Unity Township. A transcription of his will is below.

> *"In the name of God Amen. Gerhart Fisces of Unity Township in the County of Westmoreland and in the state of Pennsylvania Yeoman being very sick and weak in body but of sound mind memory and understanding thanks be for the same but considering the uncertainty of this transitory life I do make and publish this my last will and*

---

[156] Notes from J.A. and Elma Fiscus. Found in Mary Whittaker Family Tree on Ancestry.com
[157] Ibid

Testament in manner and form following. to wit principally and firstly of all I commend my immortal soul into the hands of Almight* God who gave it and my body to the Earth to be buried in a decent Christian like manner at the discretion of my Executors hereinafter (sic) named and as for the estate which it hath pleased God to blss* me in this life I give and dispose of the same in the following manner my will is that my just debts and funeral expenses be paid by my Executors. I give and bequeath unto my Elder son John Fisces the sum of five shillings for his share in case he forsake his Religion. I give and bequeath unto Adam Weaver my son in law the sum of five shillings for his share he has received two hundred pounds of my estate. I bequeath unto my son Abraham the sum of one hundred sixty three pounds whereof he must take good care of his Mother. I give and bequeath unto my Dear beloved wife Magdalena all my household goods in the kitchen and in the rooms that is to say the beds and beding* and the chest and table and all the chairs and all the casting and pewter where in the kitchen and she shall have full privilege* in the Household and in the garden and that part of the orged* which belongs to me and if there is any apples in the orged* then shall my son make sider for her and he shall have the half of the sider for his Trouble* and my said Wife shall have Every Year(illegible) income of my place in weat* and Rye and what is mentioned in a certain Article and she shall have one Cow and one calf and the spinning wheel and all the books and my Will is that my said Wife shall live on the place or along with my son. If she live [leave] the place she will forfit* all her bequeaths and all the money that is due is to come to the Executors to Ensist* my said Wife if she stands in need for it she shall have all the above mentioned articles and immediately after her decease I give and bequeath unto my son Charley Fisces and unto my [illegible] and unto John Maculough the only surviving child of my daughter Barbara the residue [illegible] this to be sold and the money to be devided* into three equal share and *share alike and lastly I nominate and appoint my son Abraham Fisces and John Hugus to be the Executors of this my Last Will and Testament revoking all other Wills and Testament Legacies and bequeathments by me heretofore made in witness whereof I have hereunto set my hand and seal this thirtieth day of September in the year of our Lord one thousand seven hundred and ninety seven.*

Published Pronounced and Declared this his Last Will and Testament. Gerhart Fiscus (signature) In the presence of us who in his presence and at his request have subscribed as witnesses: Philip Smith Jacob Shupe Proved November 4, and Recorded "

NOTE: * = sic. English was a second language to Garet and to his transcriber, so the spelling of words are written as they sounded.

Garet disposed of his estate in the following manner. John, his oldest son, received *"five shillings for his share in case he forsakes his Religion."* The purchasing power in 1797 of five shillings would be approximately one day's wage as a skilled tradesman.[158] The phrase *"lest he forsakes his Religion"* is curious.

To Adam Weaver, his son-in-law husband to Catherine Elizabeth), he left *"five shillings for his share he has received two hundred pounds of my estate."* The purchasing power of two hundred pounds in 1797 was the equivalent of 1333 days working wages of a skilled tradesman.[159]

Abraham Fiscus, his youngest son, received *"163 pounds whereof he must take good care of his mother."*

Finally, his *"…Beloved wife"* received all household goods, full use of the garden, part of the orchard, one cow and one calf, some annual income from wheat and rye, the spinning wheel and all the books. Garet says he hopes she will continue to live on the place or along with his son Abraham, but if she leaves then she will lose everything and the Executors would then provide for her.

---

[158] https://www.nationalarchives.gov.uk/currency-converter/#currency-result
[159] Ibid.

"Charley" was to receive everything Mary Magdalena had received after she dies. To John "Maculough, the only surviving child of my daughter Barbara" he leaves money from the "residue [illegible]."

Garet had always been a provider for his family, and his last will and testament shows he left them with what surely must have been considered a nice inheritance.

CHAPTER TEN

Legacy of Garet Fiscus

Gerhart Fiscus lived an extraordinary life by any measure. He epitomized the very finest of our immigrant ancestors who risked their lives to cross the Atlantic ocean and make a new life in America. Once here, many served as indentured servants before being able to forge their new lives. And most importantly, they fought for independence for their new home. These ancestors possessed courage and grit and self-sacrifice.

Documentation of Garet's life shows it was filled with daring, adventure, love, peril, war, travel, heartbreak, success, hard work, and a deep faith. He raised himself up from a poor Palatine boy and indentured servant to successful landowner and community leader in Pennsylvania. He had helped his new country, no longer the British American Colonies, become the United States of America. Garet Fiscus and his sons were true American Patriots. But of all his accomplishments, Garet's family was surely his greatest legacy.

It is an honor to be his fifth great granddaughter, through his second son, Charles.

FAMILY TREE

GARET (GERHART) FISCUS (1725 – 1797)
Married MARY MAGDALENA MERTENS

CHARLES FISCUS (1760 - 1804)
Married ZERUIA WRAY

DAVID FISCUS (1830 – 1918)
Married ANNA ROADMAN

REBECCA FISCUS LEACOCK (1822 – 1891)
Married JOSEPH BERRIE LEACOCK

WILLIAM LEACOCK (1849 – 1925)
Married AMY HOBBS

MARY LEACOCK TIETJEN (1888 – 1957)
Married ALFRED DIETRICH HERMAN TIETJEN

JULIA TIETJEN WHITTAKER (1925 – 2003)
Married LEONARD WHITTAKER

MARY WHITTAKER CRAMER (1953)
Married BRUCE CRAMER

> **JONATHAN CRAMER (1980)**
> Married KATI ROBERTSON
>
> **THOMAS CRAMER (1982)**
> Married AMANDA KIS
>
> **MICHELLE CRAMER (1984)**
> Married BRANDON LICHTI

ACKNOWLEGEMENT

I would like to acknowledge my first cousin, William Tietjen, who helped with genealogical research that documented the American Revolutionary service of Garet Fiscus and his son Charles Fiscus for The Daughters of the American Revolution (DAR).

About the Author

Mary Cramer is wife to Bruce; mother to Jonathan, Thomas, and Michelle; and grandmother to Anna, Erin, Allison, Emily, Calvin, Audenzia, and Leon (God's miracle child). She retired as Professor Emeritus from the University of Nebraska Medical Center College of Nursing in 2018 and now enjoys her time with the grandchildren, traveling, watercolor painting, genealogy, golf, and writing.

Made in the USA
Columbia, SC
30 January 2025

767bac16-5120-4577-9b7b-d81c271232cfR02